On Skis
to the North Pole

On Skis
to the North Pole

Vladimir Snegirev

Translated from the Russian
by George Watts

Sphinx Press, Inc.
New York, New York

The Publisher wishes to thank Mr. Georgi Isachenko of Novosti for suggesting the publication of this book and for his assistance, which was essential for its successful completion.

Library of Congress Cataloging in Publication Data

Snegirev, Vladimir.
  On skis to the North Pole.

  1. Snegirev, Vladimir.   2. North Pole.   I. Title.
G606.S66 1984   919.8   84-10666
ISBN 0-8236-8656-6

Manufactured in the United States of America

Contents

Author Vladimir Snegirev

In Lieu of a Prologue

On February 1, 1980, seven of my comrades, who almost a year earlier had conquered the North Pole on skis, descended the ramp of a plane at London's Heathrow Airport. They had been invited to the British capital as contenders for the International Award "For Valor in Sport."

Dmitri Shparo, chief of the expedition, alighted first, a very intense expression on his face. He was followed by Yuri Khmelevsky, Anatoli Melnikov, Vladimir Ledenev, Vadim Davydov, Vladimir Rakhmanov, and Vasili Shishkarev. I was along to cover the event for my newspaper.

Under a canopy, they were met by a crowd of photographers and TV cameramen. "Seven?" they shouted inquisitively.

Customs formalities were minimal. Five minutes and our small delegation, accompanied by taciturn bobbies

1

and agile cameramen, entered the passengers' lounge. There two young women in blazers bearing the emblem of the "For Valor in Sport" Award presented each of them a bouquet of flowers. One of the women—we knew her face from the photographs in the official booklet—was Victoria Charlton, Managing Director of the Award Committee. To the delight of the reporters, she gave Dmitri Shparo a kiss on the cheek.

"Don't pay any attention to these chaps," said Miss Charlton, pointing to the bobbies. "They're here for your protection. That's how we meet guests of honor here in London."

We had a meeting with correspondents in a special press room at Heathrow. A woman correspondent from the BBC took the microphone and the initiative into her hands.

"What did you find most difficult during your trek to the Pole?" she asked.

"Covering fifteen hundred kilometers across drifting Arctic ice," replied Dmitri Shparo.

"And why did you undertake such an unusual expedition?"

"No one had ever reached the Pole across the ice from the shores of the Eurasian continent, although quite a few attempts had been made."

"Did you encounter many dangerous situations?"

"Practically every step. You could fall into a crack appearing in the ice out of nowhere. You could be mauled by a polar bear or walrus. You could freeze to death. You could take a plunge into icy waters while crossing a patch of open water. You could be crushed by a sudden hummocking of ice."

"Mr. Shparo, what are your plans for the future?"

"We're thinking of a ski passage from the shores of the USSR across the North Pole to Canada."

The headquarters of the Award Committee was a two-room suite on the sixth floor of Grosvenor House. The "Commander" here was Mr. Warwick Charlton, an elderly, stately gentleman with a handlebar mustache; it was he who several years ago had come up with the idea of introducing the Award. With a sweeping gesture he pointed to the table, a good half of which was loaded with bottles of Russian vodka. "Especially for you," he said.

A photographer from the *Daily Mail* seemed to appear out of nowhere, camera at the ready. In all likelihood they thought the Russians would start hitting the bottle with gusto. But practically all of our team preferred Coca-Cola, while Vadim Davydov and I took a gin and tonic. Rakhmanov, due to his almost excessive modesty, refused even the Coca-Cola.

Mr. Warwick Charlton explained a few things about the Award. "A special Award Fund has been set up by various companies and banks in Great Britain and other countries. The most skillful Royal jewelers have made a laurel wreath of pure gold valued at one hundred thousand pounds sterling. It is a challenge prize. A gold copy of the wreath worth five thousand pounds is presented to the victor.

"Every year there are up to a thousand contenders for the Award from more than a hundred and twenty countries. A panel of judges made up of famous athletes, publishers, and writers selects eight to ten contenders who are invited to London, where at the beginning of February the victors are chosen and crowned."

In the morning after breakfast, we descended to the lounge.

"Hey," Rakhmanov whispered, "Isn't that Japanese fellow over there Uemura?"

Everyone turned to look at the only man ever to conquer the North Pole alone. Last year, the valiant Japanese had been awarded the gold wreath for this exploit, and now he was in London to pass on the Award to his successor.

It seemed that someone had pointed Shparo out to Uemura in the same way. The Japanese sportsman, smiling broadly, was headed straight for us. Dmitri went to meet him. In the middle of the lounge the two polar explorers embraced in a bear hug. The room seemed to glow with sincerity, goodwill, and restrained courage.

Each of us knew in detail about the amazing journeys of Naomi Uemura, his daring trek to the Pole by dogsled. And he had heard about our expedition. In June of 1979 he had cabled us his congratulations.

Later on, we had a chance to speak with him in his suite. He is something of a character. Trying to pick the correct English words, he drags out "eh-eh-eh" and looks up at the ceiling. In some ways he is quite eccentric; for example, when we were posing for a group photograph in front of the hotel, Uemura sat himself down in a pose right on the pavement.

He told us about his journey to the Pole, which took fifty-four days—March 6 to April 29, 1978. He set out from Cape Columbia on a pine sled drawn by a team of seventeen huskies. On seven occasions Canadian planes dropped parcels of food for him and his dogs. One day he was almost mauled by a polar bear that ripped open his tent and ate up his stock of food. But even conquering the Pole did not seem to satisfy Uemura. Once there, he flew immediately back to the mainland and, without even a day's rest, harnessed another sled and drove his dogs all the way across Greenland—from Cape Morris Jesup in the north to its southernmost tip. He covered a distance of about three thousand kilometers in a little over a hundred days.

"Was your expedition to the Pole the most dangerous thing you've attempted?" I asked.

"Yes, of course," Uemura energetically nodded; "as

well as my solitary ascents of the highest mountain peaks on all the continents, and my raft voyage down the Amazon from the Peruvian Andes to the Atlantic, when the only food I ate was bananas and piranhas—and the piranhas," Uemura laughed, "were just waiting until I made a false move so as to gobble me up."

"It's difficult even to imagine such dangerous expeditions," said Melnikov. That was just like him.

"But the fact that you Russians made it to the Pole on skis is even more difficult to imagine. But you did it."

"Mr. Uemura, why did you go to the Pole alone?"

"What about the dogs, don't they count?" he said, betraying no irony whatsoever, and then continued: "Living in a collective, in my experience, is always fraught with quarrels: one man wants one thing, another wants the exact opposite. These contradictions are not for me. I don't ask the dogs what they want."

"Do you mean to say you always travel alone?"

"Always alone! That's my style. Ten years ago I scaled Mt. Everest with a group, but it wasn't for me. I want to be the first, and do not wish to share the limelight with anyone. But if I ever make an exception to this rule, it will be to make a joint expedition with you. We could, say, make a journey by dogsled from Cape Dezhnev to Scandinavia."

Guildhall is one of the oldest public buildings in London. Decorated with bas-relief that has aged with time, its ancient walls have witnessed eight centuries of pomp and splendor. The people gathered here today are about to honor the contenders for the Award "For Valor in Sport." Besides the Committee, the contenders, and the judges, the ceremony is attended by British Lords, the ambassadors of several nations, functionaries of the international sports movement, and celebrities from all over the world. Throngs of correspondents, photographers, and cameramen are covering the ceremony, which is being telecast to fifty countries.

Between bringing us food and drinks, the waiters come by our table with the Award booklets, in which, along with pictures of the other contenders, there is a photo of the *Komsomolskaya Pravda* Polar Expedition. "Your autographs, please," they ask us.

At last, it seems, the luncheon is over. By now the hall is uncomfortably warm, what with the merciless floodlights the TV crews have brought in. It doesn't help that everyone is sitting on pins and needles awaiting the results of the voting.

As we sip old port, the Lord Mayor of London begins the round of speeches. He is followed on the podium by Victoria Charlton and the official statement by Uemura ("It is easier for me to kill a bear than to say two phrases in English," is how he begins.) Next the judges are presented, and then, finally, the moment we have all been waiting for: Mr. Warwick Charlton rises to his feet.

"Ladies and gentlemen," he intones, "allow me to give you the names of the contenders for the Award 'For Valor in Sport,' and to introduce them to you. Valor is difficult to define in words, but all of us easily recognize it when we see it in life. Valor is that supreme ability of the human spirit and reason to dauntlessly overcome every obstacle and difficulty. It is that self-sacrifice which may, in equal degree, be attributed to both victor and vanquished."

As he reads each name, the person rises from his seat and the entire hall applauds him.

First, the world recordholder for deep sea diving without a breathing apparatus, Jacques Mayol. The Frenchman rises and bows most elegantly. He is fifty-one years old, a truly sociable person. In a chat with the Soviet skiers, he spoke at length about his diving secrets. He calls himself a dolphin. His record, which he set after training for fifteen years, is almost beyond belief: in three minutes, forty seconds, he "swam" to a depth of one hundred meters and back, all without a breathing apparatus of any kind.

The next name to be called is that of Dean Chenoweth, a forty-two-year-old American from Florida. We also managed to make friends with this man, who bears himself modestly and seems to go almost unnoticed: yesterday we supped together at one table, and had a long chat. Dean became famous for his daring attempt to eclipse the world speed record on water. For thirty long years he advanced toward his goal, designing and building speedboats. His last boat, outfitted with an engine from an Australian B-51 bomber, looked like a giant scooter. He undertook his attempt with this boat on October 23, 1979.

On Lake Washington near Seattle, Dean was to accelerate for two miles, and then zip through a one-mile control sector at a speed exceeding Roy Duby's world record of 201 miles per hour. At the beginning, everything was going perfectly: the boat entered the control sector at a speed of 220 miles per hour. But at the halfway mark the propeller began to disintegrate for some reason, causing powerful vibrations and then an explosion. Dean was blasted out of the cockpit and the remnants of his hydroplane flew up in the air, made a loop, and then smacked down on the water. When he came to an hour and a half later in the hospital, Dean discovered he had eight broken ribs, internal injuries, and a fractured pelvis. The official bulletin read: "No one in the world could survive after striking the water at that speed." But he did survive. And yesterday at supper, he told us that he was soon going to take another crack at the record; because he failed to complete the mile, his performance was thrown out.

Next the French hang-glider pilot, Jean-Marc Boivin, is presented. Curly-haired and handsome, this twenty-nine-year-old from Dijon once worked as a mountain guide; when he took a liking to hang-gliders, he decided to set the world record by sailing from the peak of K-2 in the Himalayas, 7,600 meters high. The ascent to the peak took Boivin four months. The weather was vicious, and the expedition he was with had selected a route hitherto unconquered by climbers. Besides his knapsack with personal belongings and food, he also carried a twenty-kilogram hang-glider.

On the way to the top, the Frenchman lost most of his vision, and his fingers were frostbitten. Tired and exhausted at the summit he had not lost his desire to make the return trip by air. His companions helped him assemble the glider. Boivin waved to them . . . and took a step into the chasm. For the first few seconds he plummeted downward with the speed of a falling rock; the rarefied air gave no support to his wings. But in seven seconds his speed had dropped to fifty miles an hour. It was only with great difficulty that he could make out even the contour of the mountains surrounding him; his frostbitten fingers could hardly feel the controls. Thirty minutes later, Boivin had landed safely at the foot of K-2.

"I now call upon Dmitri Shparo and his six valiant companions," Mr. Warwick Charlton solemnly announces.

The audience bursts into applause. Hundreds of people turn to look at my comrades. I cannot say for sure, but it seems to me the ovation for the Soviet skiers is the longest of all.

During the past three days, the London newspapers covering our visit seemed, whether they intended it or not, to be inculcating the idea that the Soviet skiers were the most worthy contenders. To be quite frank, we too believed in the possibility of victory. My friends realized full well that they were no better than the other contenders, but nevertheless . . . nevertheless. . . . Only Khmelevsky, who was true to his habit of analyzing everything, held a dissenting opinion. "No, it's a lost cause," he insisted. Last year the Award went to Uemura for conquering the North Pole, and they won't be presenting it for the same exploit two years in a row."

All of us nodded our heads in agreement and . . . continued to believe in Lady Luck.

Finally—finally—the last act of the three-hour ceremony at Guildhall: Mr. Warwick Charlton, his voice quavering with emotion, makes the announcement: "The gold laurel wreath, by decision of the judges, is awarded to. . . ."

It was so quiet in the huge hall you could hear a pin drop.

". . . French sportsman, Jean-Marc Boivin!"

The smiling Frenchman, nimbly threading his way through the tables, mounts the stage to receive the Award. He receives a standing ovation. Very solemnly, the gold wreath is placed on his head. He is warmly congratulated by Naomi Uemura, and the members of the Soviet delegation come up to congratulate him.

That's it. The ceremony is over. We come out on the square in front of Guildhall. A winter rain—warm to us Muscovites—has left puddles shining on the pavement; a heart-gladdening sun has peeked out from behind the clouds. Turning our faces sunward, we stand there a few moments and—strange—none of us has the slightest feeling of disappointment. I can see that quite clearly.

"The main thing is not victory but the attempt—isn't that right?" says Ledenev, an ear-to-ear smile on his face.

Miss Victoria Charlton approaches us.

"If you only knew how stormy yesterday's voting was," she said, a note of guilt in her voice. "You were only one vote short of victory. . . ."

"Don't worry, Victoria. Next time, we'll win for sure." This is Vasili, trying to reassure her. "The lunch in Guildhall was delicious; we hope to try it again."

Spellbound by the Desert of Ice

When did it start? Ten, eleven years ago? I can tell you exactly: June 3, 1969. It was on this hot summer day in Moscow that we took our first step toward the North Pole.

Summer that year had come early. Already by June it was dry, and the sun beat down mercilessly day after day. The white fluff of poplars, together with the muted noise of traffic from the baking streets below, came floating through the open windows of the *Komsomolskaya Pravda* offices. A stillness had set in all over the city, it seemed, everything torpid from the heat wave. Even the usual newspaper hustle and bustle had slowed to a crawl. We all sat languidly at our desks, cursing the heat and dreaming of nightfall.

The next moment, or an emblem of it, stands fixed in my memory: all of a sudden a gust of cold air seemed to fill the office, as if somehow, incongruously, a blizzard

11

were raging all about us. Two young men, strangers to all of us, had entered the room.

"Dmitri Shparo," announced the first one, stepping forward confidently. He was tall, dark-haired, slim but well-proportioned. His dark eyes had a penetrating look, with not even a trace of the awkwardness or diffidence so often encountered in people who for the first time find themselves in the offices of a national publication like ours. Our guest was wearing a well-cut grey suit which, to be honest, seemed a bit baggy on his slight frame.

"Yuri Khmelevsky," came a second voice, this one much quieter than the first, but very casual-sounding. It belonged to a thick-set, broad-shouldered young man wearing thick glasses. His clothing matched his voice for casualness: black, almost shabby slacks held up by a cracked old leather belt, a poorly ironed white shirt, and shoes with long, droopy laces that threatened to untie themselves at any moment.

The faces of both men glowed in splotches of a strange, almost cherry-red color we were quick to notice, as if their features had been unevenly heated by a strong flame.

"That's the wind and the sun," Shparo explained; "that's how they worked over our faces." Our perplexed stares had not been lost on him. "The *Arctic* sun and wind," he was quick to specify.

Together with three of their friends, it developed, these young men had trekked on skis the three hundred kilometers from the city of Vorkuta, above the Arctic Circle, to the town of Amderma on the shores of the Arctic Ocean. On their journey they had endured blizzards, fights with polar bears, temperatures as low as minus fifty degrees Centigrade, with only a frail tent for shelter, and magnetic storms that rendered their compasses useless. Now, three hundred kilometers may not seem a great distance, yet these city-dwellers, Muscovites all of them,

12

had covered the distance across snow-filled tundra, without snowmobiles or dogsleds, relying only on their own strength and courage. They had no special equipment, no fur-lined clothing, no radio transmitter. They used ordinary department-store skis, ate ordinary tinned beef, drank ordinary Georgian tea. Not one of them was a professional polar explorer. Shparo and Khmelevsky were themselves both mathematicians, while the rest of their party comprised a physicist, a radio engineer, and a designer of hydroelectric stations.

Intrigued, we invited them to prepare their diary for publication in *Komsomolskaya Pravda*. They accepted readily, but seemed in no hurry to leave. Khmelevsky had a vacant look on his face, while Shparo knitted his brows. He seemed to be looking for a way to switch the subject to more important matters.

"We have an idea," he said finally. "Here it is: we propose that the editorial offices of *Komsomolskaya Pravda* organize a permanent voluntary polar expedition, using our group as its nucleus."

Shparo fell silent, giving us a chance to digest the proposal. Our newspaper sponsor a polar expedition? Why, we asked ourselves; to what end? And to what possible benefit? Frankly, the proposal struck us on first hearing as utterly wild.

But Shparo by now was waxing enthusiastic. "Yes, yes," he exuded, "a polar expedition sponsored by *Komsomolskaya Pravda*. The newspaper's backing would allow us to operate at a much higher level. Just imagine the routes! We could go by skis to the Taimyr Peninsula. We'd make it to the glaciers of the Arctic archipelagoes. And maybe we'd even embark on a trip across drifting icefloes! And *Komsomolskaya Pravda* would be able to cover it all. A story like this is bound to be of interest to your readers."

Now it was Khmelevsky's turn. "Such an expedition," he began, speaking with greater reserve than his friend, and taking a somewhat different tack, "could pursue a whole series of unique scientific investigations." He was speaking very precisely, testing each word as if it were a treacherous piece of ice he was about to set foot on. "For example: geographical observations in remote areas above the Arctic Circle could be quite useful. And medical science might well be interested in studying the physiological changes observed in a group making an arduous journey through Arctic regions. In short, the expedition would be a scientific undertaking as well as a sporting one."

Shparo and Khmelevsky gave us plenty to think about on a sultry afternoon. One thing was certain: no Soviet newspaper had ever organized a polar expedition. How was it done? Where to begin? We needed time to think it over and agreed to meet our unexpected visitors in a few days. Perhaps then we could give them a more definite answer.

When they had gone, I remember we sat in silence for a long time. But this was no longer the result of torpor. Pretty soon a map was brought out, and we all began poring over it. There was the dotted line of the Arctic Circle, over here the huge Taimyr Peninsula, like a hibernating bear. There to the west were strung the islands of Franz Josef Land, and there, at the center of everything, stood the Pole. The names themselves were enough to evoke long-forgotten romantic associations—the stories of Jack London, the landscapes of Rockwell Kent—and we almost shivered just thinking of that endless desert of ice, the howling wind, and the cold.

The mysterious Arctic. Without knowing anything about it, I could feel its strong attraction. I recalled the shining eyes of Shparo and Khmelevsky, spellbound by the desert of ice, and their words: "On the fifteenth day of the journey we emerged on the shores of the Kara Sea. The ice hummocks were blue and seemed piled to the sky."

14

SPELLBOUND BY THE DESERT OF ICE

As time went by, Dmitri and Yuri dropped into our offices more and more frequently, gradually getting everyone accustomed to the idea that we simply had to sponsor a permanent expedition. In the spring of 1970 they embarked on another journey, this time carrying *Komsomolskaya Pravda* vouchers—such was our modest support at the beginning. That year the five skiers covered a distance of five hundred kilometers from Lake Taimyr to the northernmost tip of the Eurasian continent—Cape Chelyuskin. The published accounts of this adventure were enthusiastically received. The time was ripe, we concluded, and 1970 saw the establishment of the permanent expedition.

The next journey would be made on skis across Severnaya Zemlya, a group of islands locked in ice and snow to the north of Taimyr. A successful expedition to this archipelago, the least explored and most severe stretch of land in all the Arctic, offered the possibility of undertaking still more daring treks. Failure could mean irreparable tragedy.

This time I was included in preparations for the journey. Shparo, chief of the expedition, agreed to this, bearing in mind that I was born in Siberia and was not a bad skier. But the main thing that convinced him was my promise to become a radio operator in the shortest possible time. Before this, the expedition had carried no radio equipment.

So, after my working day was over at the newspaper, I would hurry to the Central Radio Club to master the ABCs of radio communications and to learn Morse code. In addition, several times a week I participated in various physical training exercises with the rest of the team and worked with them in getting our equipment ready. At the same time, I pursued a task I had set myself: before heading north to learn more about practical work under polar conditions, I had determined to read everything I could find by Arctic explorers. I must admit that I tackled this

15

job most eagerly; these books, consisting mostly of diaries, proved absolutely fascinating. They were stories of restrained courage and of nobility, of love of the frozen North, of disappointment and of sorrow. I came away from them convinced that anyone wishing to experience genuine purposefulness, undaunted spirit, and real adventure must read the diaries of Nansen and Scott, Papanin and Ushakov, Peary and Begounek.

While reading through the notes of Robert Scott, who together with his companions perished tragically in the Antarctic on the way back to their base camp from the South Pole, I came across the following entry: "From my point of view, not a single journey by dogsled can yield such results as a mission whose participants overcome difficulties, danger and hardships, relying only on their own strength, spending days and weeks in hard physical labor so as to fathom some of the mysteries of the great unknown. Without a doubt, in the latter case victory is attained in a more noble way, and shines more brilliantly." I copied these words into a notebook and showed them to Dmitri the next time he stopped by.

"We could easily take these words for our motto," he said. "Some people think the time for exotic voyages is past, that in this age of jets and atomic icebreakers there is no need to go by foot. But that is not true; the words of Robert Scott hold true even today. To fathom the mysteries of the great unknown—remote regions, man himself, his capabilities—for this there is no substitute for expeditions on skis or on foot."

Shparo was evidently warming to his topic. "Skis," he went on, "are a very natural means of travel for man. In the North they are indispensable. Dogsleds, they're a thing of the past. Snowmobiles are good, but you can't go everywhere on them. Skis are convenient, simple, dependable. Right now man is actively settling the Arctic and starting to develop it economically, and our experi-

16

ence on skiing expeditions will benefit geologists, other polar explorers, and anyone compelled to make a forced landing in the tundra. Am I right?"

How could I not agree? At that time I lived as in a dream.

One of the rooms at the *Komsomolskaya Pravda* offices began to look like a warehouse. Crates of canned goods were stacked to the ceiling. Several sleds, extra strong skis made especially for the expedition, tents, sleeping bags, fur-lined socks, mittens, wool sweaters, parkas, portable oil stoves, theodolites—there seemed no end to the items we had to take along. The newspaper staff dropped by all day long to take a look at the sleds, to ask about our route, to taste our rations. Most of the food had been freeze-dried and sealed in tinfoil—meat, cottage cheese, even strawberries. The advantages were obvious: a lightweight, easy to prepare, and conveniently packaged product.

We organized tasting sessions right in the office: any-one could drop in to taste dehydrated cottage cheese with blackcurrant paste and dehydrated sausage. The "con-noisseurs," of course, were disappointed: conventional products are doubtless more tasty. In Severnaya Zemlya, however, this cottage cheese and sausage would become our favorite dish.

At this time our contacts with various institutes and agencies became more regular. The Institute of Medico-Biological Research of the USSR Health Ministry imme-diately took a great interest in our plans. On the instruc-tions of Oleg Gazenko, the Institute's director and a prominent specialist in aerospace medicine, a research program was drawn up for us—a program that was to be continued right up to our final assault on the Pole.

Next, all of us had to go through a painstaking med-ical examination at the Institute. This was to provide back-ground data for subsequent research. First we underwent a battery of psychological tests. At one point each of us was isolated in a pressure chamber and asked to cancel out certain combinations of light signals by pressing buttons. Another test had us quickly detecting pairs of different colored numbers on a screen and calling them out—even numbers at the beginning of the row, odd numbers at the end. This was not always so simple, especially with the examiner sitting behind you, monotonously mumbling out his numbers so as to distract you. It was only by sheer willpower that you kept yourself from turning around and telling the examiner where to get off.

Then the clinicians tackled us: venal blood test, finger blood, gastric juice analysis, ECG, vision test . . . Surgeon, psychiatrist, neuropathologist, more venal blood, more analyses.

Clearly, as we prepared for a fascinating and difficult expedition, these specialists were preparing an interesting and unique experiment.

The five hundred kilometer trek across Severnaya Zemlya won my heart to the Arctic forever—I was hopelessly in love. Finally I could feel for myself the powerful magnetic force of the white wilderness, and knew I had reached a turning point in my life. The feeling was exhilarating. For the expedition, Severnaya Zemlya became a kind of touchstone. It was quite clear to us that the time had come to plan a sortie out onto the drifting ice. More and more often when maps were out, I would catch my friends eyeing that coveted point: the North Pole.

In 1972 the expedition first ventured out onto the open sea: we decided to "test" the icefloes in Long Strait, which separates Chukchi Peninsula from Wrangel Island. I need not go into the details here—there will be plenty of opportunity to return to them in the course of the story. Suffice it to say that after our successful crossing of Long Strait the group embarked on a training expedition across the New Siberian Islands. This was followed by a series of summer expeditions to the Taimyr Peninsula and the Kara Sea, for the purpose of carrying out studies in historical geography. In 1976 the group became the first in the world to ski from the mainland—Wrangel Island, actually—to the drifting scientific observatory NP-23. Finally came 1979 and permission to start for the top of the planet.

These were years of hard training and diligent preparation. Equipment had to be designed, many elements of which were unique. Each journey brought the expedition more acclaim. Prominent scientists began referring to the results of our observations and discoveries, and our practical recommendations became the basis for a number of Arctic survival manuals. However, our main accomplishment during these years was the molding of a close-knit group of comrades geared to a common goal. For each of us, the trek to the Pole was not only an objective for the immediate future, but a treasured part of life.

Speaking candidly, the group was in good shape and could have departed for the Pole much sooner than 1979. However, we had to prove this not only to ourselves but also to those who had the final say in the matter. To many people, the very idea of skiing to the North Pole seemed unusual, even fantastic. It took years to convince them that our plan was realistic, to prove that such an undertaking was both possible and necessary.

And not all of us withstood this test of time. Of those who were with the expedition at the very beginning, only two remained—Shparo and Khmelevsky. I must admit that there were moments when I too had doubts as to the ultimate success of the project. There was only one among us who never, under any circumstances, fell into despair, whose radiant optimism was our staunchest support: Dmitri Shparo. I have known him now for years, and hardly a day goes by that we do not see each other or at least speak on the phone. Nevertheless, I continue to discover new qualities in his character, and never cease to wonder at his dynamic energy. He is the very model of purposefulness and organization. No one has ever seen him sitting in idleness; phones are forever ringing around him. It would seem that from birth he was "programmed" to work without respite, and he drives himself and those around him without letup.

Psychology distinguishes "nominal" leaders, those who by virtue of their position within a formal hierarchy stand above the rest, from "real" leaders—persons of true authority. With the help of sophisticated tests and special devices, psychology claims the ability to quite accurately identify these dynamic individuals. However, it was not psychology but life itself, the very logistics of forming a collective, that projected Shparo into a position of leadership. No one appointed him chief of the expedition; it simply became evident that he had become so, with the tacit consent of us all.

In the sixties, when there was not as yet a permanent expedition, simply a group of enthusiasts, recent university graduates, there was no leader. They simply went on hikes to the Ural Mountains and the Kola Peninsula, to the Sayan Mountains and Mt. Elbrus. But the more complicated the routes, the clearer the goals, the more apparent became the need for a distribution of duties and responsibilities. So when the question of expedition chief finally came up, no one could imagine anyone but Dmitri in that slot. Even at that time, he had already developed the authority of a true leader.

As chief of the expedition, Shparo has but one privilege: he always goes first. First to rise in the morning, first to shoulder his rucksack, first to arrive for training sessions (and always the last to leave). Whether in Moscow or in the North, he spares himself nothing.

"Do you know the secret of his energy?" Khmelevsky asked me one day. "Every person, sooner or later, reaches the end of his rope, the limit of psychological endurance.

There comes a time when all of us reach this point and seem to give in. But Dmitri will keep on pushing himself beyond that point, as long as he is conscious."

Dmitri himself speaks of this in a somewhat different way. "I am afraid," he says, "that I will not manage to do everything I am capable of."

I must confess that at times I have felt something closely akin to enmity toward Dmitri. During such moments I see something callous in him, and seem to hear the whirr of an automaton. There are situations, after all, in which it is quite natural for a human being to be at a loss, to blush, to display some weakness; it is all this that makes a person human. But Dmitri will never so much as stumble over a word while making an important report; he will never blush while being introduced to a young lady who has caught his fancy. For ten hours a day he will pound his typewriter on the shores of a southern sea amid all the temptations of vacation time. And even proposing a New Year's toast, he is almost sure to fire some sharp barb at any negligent member of the expedition.

Sometimes I rebuke him for his excessive rationalism, and by intentionally sharp remarks try to engage him in an argument about it. Invariably, however, my remarks are met with utter incomprehension—you would think we were from different planets.

False modesty is absolutely alien to Shparo. Once, when we were all filling in a questionnaire, one of the questions was the following: do you think your expedition would exist without its chief? To this Dmitri gave the following reply: "Probably not, because in many vitally important matters no one can take his place. As time goes by, there is a tendency for the group to be distracted from the orbit of the expedition (family matters, careers, and so on); that is why it is necessary to develop a strong, ever more powerful magnetic pull toward the center. By his new ideas, Shparo generates this magnetic force, both naturally and artificially."

This reply might well have struck the person who compiled the questionnaire as immodest. However, it cannot be denied that everyone who knows Shparo well would consider it entirely truthful. I cannot say that his candor and his bustling activity are to everyone's liking. Certainly there are many who feel uncomfortable in his presence. Well, so much the worse for them.

A senior lecturer and Candidate in Physico-Mathematical Sciences, Dmitri teaches at Moscow's Institute of Steel and Alloys. He sits on the bureau of the Polar Regions Department under the Moscow branch of the Geographical Society. He organizes scientific conferences and is a contributing editor of *Pravda*, penning critical articles on problems of higher education. He is also deputy chairman of his Institute's Physical Training and Sports Commission, directing his energies to such projects as the construction of a swimming pool and organizing cross-country races for the students.

At home he has a wife and two sons he must also make time for. Three times a week there are grueling training sessions with all the members of the expedition, and every day he receives letters from all parts of the country, not one of which goes unanswered.

The questionnaire mentioned earlier also contained the following question: what made you participate in the expedition? "A sense of duty before the ultimate objective of conquering the Pole," replied Dmitri. "To me, it is a patriotic task. I am influenced also by the expedition's tremendous possibilities—scientific, sporting, educative —its collective spirit."

Do you smoke? drink? inquired the questionnaire. "I do not smoke. I smoked while studying at the Institute, but I dropped the habit in my sophomore year. Now I simply hate smoking. How can a person intentionally destroy his health? I value life too much—the expedition, my family, books, creativity—to consciously rob myself in this manner. And I drink almost nothing. As the years go by the pleasures of drinking diminish for me, while the drawbacks are felt much more strongly."

During the entire period of the expedition's existence, not a single event occurred that could be called an accident. And what punishing treks had been made! I credit this to Dmitri's thoroughness, his passion for organization; when preparing an expedition, he seems to take into account everything that might possibly happen. His credo is check and *triple* check.

And triple doggedness!

I recall the summer of 1977, a tiny island in the Kara Sea. Snow flurries are followed by cold, biting rain. Huge chunks of pack ice nuzzle up to the rocky shores. Night has fallen. In a deserted hunter's cabin we stoke the stove till it becomes red-hot. We are the base camp group and sit basking in the warmth—some in our bunks, others on the floor—awaiting this evening's radio contact with the mobile groups. The goal of our summer work in the Kara Sea is to find the traces of the schooner *Hercules*, which perished somewhere in this area around the turn of the century. Its crew, under the command of the Russian polar explorer, Vladimir Rusanov, who was attempting to sail from Atlantic to Pacific by way of the North coast, met their death somewhere along these shores. For several years now we have been trying to solve the mystery of this Arctic tragedy. Now our expedition has divided itself into four mobile teams in order to make a thorough search of the island.

Those of us who have remained at the base camp have the job of maintaining radio contact with the other groups, while our scuba divers examine the seabed where the *Hercules* is thought to have gone down. This is our second week on the island, but still the divers have not begun their work: in their way stands an ice shelf two meters thick. In spite of the August weather it still stub-

23

bornly clings to the shore. Only a storm could carry it out to sea, yet there are no indications whatever that one is approaching. Another possibility is that the shelf might be melted by the August sun, but it has rarely peeked out from behind the dark grey clouds that are prevailing.

Speaking over the radio in a hopeless tone, the chief of the scuba divers, Stanislav Prapor, explains the situation to Dmitri. And we hear Shparo's categorical reply: "I propose that you destroy the ice with all available means."

Prapor shrugs his shoulders in bewilderment, and looks at us, seeking support. He has long ago decided for himself that nothing can be done. "The ice where we must dive is two meters thick," he again explains to us. "A pickax is no good. It'll take us until winter to chop through it."

Radio operator Georgi Ivanov nods his head in agreement and switches on the receiver. All is quiet in the cabin—everyone is waiting to hear what Shparo will say.

The chief's voice, distorted by static, sounds a bit peeved: "There are no insurmountable obstacles for the Komsomolskaya Pravda polar expedition!"

So in the morning we got down to a job which, if viewed from the sidelines, seems absurd in the extreme (a crowbar and pickax against polar ice?!). We grappled with the ice shelf one day, two days, three days. . . . At first we were assisted by the wind and the waves, and then by the sun's rays. By the fifth day nothing was left of the ice. And then came the moment when the divers donned their wetsuits and tanks and slipped into the dark waters of the Kara Sea. But that is another story.

Mankind turned its gaze toward the Pole almost as soon as it became known that the earth was a sphere. Today science explains the first attempts to reach the northern latitudes by the desire of ancient seafarers to find a shorter

contribution to our knowledge of the North, and expanded our conception of the limits of human endurance and possibilities.

A meeting of all those involved in the polar expedition was held at the *Komsomolskaya Pravda* offices in January 1979, a month and a half before our departure to the Arctic. Chairing the meeting was the newspaper's Editor-in-Chief, Valeri Ganichev, and represented there were the civil aviation department, State Committee of the USSR for Hydrometeorology and Environmental Protection, the North Coast Route Administration, several research organizations, Voluntary Society for Collaboration with the Army, Air Force, and Navy, and the Central Committee of the Young Communist League. As Executive Secretary of the permanent expedition, I announced the agenda, the purpose of which was to check one last time the readiness of the expedition for carrying out its mission. Then the floor was yielded to Dmitri Shparo. After making his formal introductory remarks, he plunged into the details of the program, and introduced the participants.

"Altogether, there will be twelve men in the expedition—seven on the ski team and five in the support group. Besides myself, the ski team will include Yuri Khmelevsky, chief of scientific research and navigator; Anatoli Melnikov, radio operator; Vladimir Ledenev, quartermaster and cameraman; Vadim Davydov, physician; Vladimir Rakhmanov, second navigator; and Vasili Shishkarev, second radio operator. The support group, headed by Leonid Labutin, senior radio operator of the expedition, includes Fyodor Sklokin and Georgi Ivanov, radio operators, as well as the ski team substitutes, Mikhail Deyev and Alexander Shatokhin.

"Our plan calls for the joint arrival of all the participants at the settlement of Tiksi. From there we will be shuttled to Kotelny Island in the New Siberians, where we intend to set up the base radio station of the expedition, which will be in direct communications with Moscow. Labutin and Deyev will work at this base. Sklokin's group—himself, Ivanov, and Shatokhin—will leave Kotelny for the NP-24 drifting station, which at the moment is approximately three hundred kilometers north of the New Siberian Islands. There we will set up the second radio station, less powerful, for direct contact with the skiers. Sklokin is also responsible for packing the cargo that is to be dropped to the ski team. During the drop, the aircraft will use NP-24 as an intermediate landing strip. After the work is completed at these bases, the ski team will fly out to the starting point."

Dmitri picked up a pointer and indicated a tiny spot on the map: "Right here, Henrietta Island, to the east of the New Siberians. The distance from Henrietta Island to the Pole is fifteen hundred kilometers. We plan to cover this route in seventy-two days. Our schedule will be the following. We ski for approximately two weeks and then bivouac for two days. At this point aircraft will drop the containers with food, fuel, and batteries for the next two weeks. Altogether, there wil be four such drops.

"We plan to reach the Pole during the last days of May. From there, the group will be brought back to the mainland by plane."

"Are there any questions for Dmitri Shparo?" Ganichev asked.

There were plenty. What are the skis made of? How did you train? What is the temperature in the area of the New Siberian Islands now? How do you plan to cross patches of open water and cracks in the ice? What will the skiing team eat? How dependable is the communications system? What means have been provided for distress signals and rescue operations? Dmitri gave a thorough reply to each question.

"What I want to ask," said a representative from one

of the scientific establishments, "is what are the chances of the ski team's utilizing local food resources?"

The experienced polar explorers in the room made an effort to hide their smiles. "From the practical point of view," answered Khmelevsky, "the chances are nil. On drifting ice, especially near open water, you may meet a polar bear or a walrus, but they are protected species and hunting them is forbidden. That is why the members of the expedition will have to carry their entire stock of food in their rucksacks. The main requirement these products must meet is minimum content of water and residue. The team's rations include dehydrated meat, dehydrated cottage cheese, clarified butter, salt pork, dehydrated sausage, buckwheat, oatmeal, rye rusks, biscuits, sugar, chocolate, coffee, salt, and tea. The daily intake of calories will be about fifty-five hundred calories. This will occasion a daily energy deficit of fifteen hundred calories, a deficit that will be totally compensated during the days of rest. The total energy loss during the trek should not exceed thirty-five thousand kilocalories, which is quite permissible. What this boils down to is that during the entire expedition each member will lose no more than four or five kilos of body weight."

By this point the meeting had been in session for three hours and everyone seemed satisfied. Nothing now could prevent adoption of the main resolution. After ten long years of preparation, I could hardly believe I was hearing the words I now pronounced: "Resolved that the expedition is ready to carry out its mission to reach the geographic North Pole from the shores of the USSR by skis. The day of departure of the expedition from Moscow to Tiksi will be March 1 of the current year."

Encounter with the Furious North

On March 1, as planned, a heavy cargo plane airlifted us and all our freight to the small Yakut settlement of Tiksi, at the mouth of the Lena River. Total elapsed time: twelve hours. From Tiksi we were to move in small groups further north. Though it was not far to Kotelny Island—only a two-hour flight—a blizzard there had buried the landing strip at Temp Bay under a thick blanket of snow. Nothing could land until a tractor had cleared the airstrip. Not until March 4 did our first party arrive there, when Oleg Okhonsky, captain of the IL-14 assigned to shuttle us to the island, executed a beautiful touchdown on the still friable gravel shoal that serves for an airstrip.

Kotelny Island, as large as some European states, is one of the most desolate places on earth. Here there are two small polar stations—a radio-navigation facility operated by the USSR Merchant Fleet Ministry (this is where our base camp would be) and the winter quarters of a few hunters. The stations are separated from each other by several hundred kilometers. The facility at Temp Bay consists of nothing but the landing strip, two wooden cabins, and a three-man staff. The permanent population of the island does not exceed fifty persons.

The winter here seems never to end. For ten months of the year the hilly tundra lies under a mantle of snow: a harsh and far-off land indeed.

What follows are extracts from a diary I kept on Kotelny Island.

March 5. Really cold! Minus forty-three Centigrade and a razor-sharp wind. And this is March! For the first time in many years, my faithful Kiev camera has let me down: the shutter froze. And the weather forecast for the next few days says the mercury will drop to minus fifty. Even the Eskimo dogs, which spend the whole year outdoors, at night try to sneak into the entrances of our cabins, where it is a bit warmer.

As dusk falls the northern lights begin playing in the cold sky—a spellbinding, fantastic spectacle. As if some extraterrestrial were trying to signal us or—just as mysteriously—to entertain us. The northern lights are sometimes called the "smile of the Arctic." They are considered a good omen for those embarking on a journey.

The IL-14 has already shuttled between Tiksi and Temp Bay four times, delivering more than eight tons of cargo. Now all these boxes, crates, and bags must be transported across the wintry tundra from the airstrip to the radio-navigation station, or RNS. Thirty-two kilometers is but a small hop on the mainland, but here another set of standards applies: a tractor hauling a heavy sled moves at almost a snail's pace for some five hours along a snow track marked with empty oil drums from Temp Bay to our base camp.

March 5. . . . On this day sixty-five years ago Georgi

32

Sedov (1877–1914) met his death in the Arctic ice. Sedov was the only Russian to challenge the North Pole during the big boom in polar exploration, when explorers from many countries rushed to be the first to reach the "top of the world."

Sixty-five years ago, no less than today, this land was held in the firm grip of bitter frost. Dogsleds bounced across the bumpy, snow-covered hummocks past Franz Josef Land, the packed snow squeaking like glass dust under the runners. The huskies yelped and howled. Besides this, nothing broke the silence that embraced the icy hills and the ice-bound sea.

On one of the sleds—the third and last—sprawled across the packs, lay the figure of a man. His eyes were closed, his breathing rapid and hot. For many days he had listened to the monotonous sound of the runners on the snow. He tried not to look at the wearisome coastline garbed in ice and snow. It would only immerse him further in his despair.

For years Sedov had directed his efforts toward this expedition, and he had overcome many obstacles. Now only one, final barrier stood in his way: a thousand kilometers of virgin Arctic ice. A thousand kilometers . . . and at the end of that grueling trek stood only an imaginary point, one that existed only on the map—the North Pole.

He must reach the Pole. He must! The Russian flag will fly over the top of the earth. Even if he is ill. Even if there is little food, and the kerosene is running out. But he has an iron will! He must make it to the Pole. But what is that? Why have the sleds stopped? Why is there so much fear in the eyes of the person bending over him? Oh, yes, these ordinary sailors think he is ill, and they fear for him. They try to talk him into returning to the ship. Never!

Sedov often lost consciousness. When he came to, the first thing he would do was to get out his compass and check their route. And when he saw that the dogs were heading due north, he would calm down somewhat. Whenever they stopped to rest, his companions, the young sailors Grigori Linnik and Shura Pustoshny, would frown and say, "We should go back." "No," Sedov replied each time. "No, and forget about it." And then, again slipping into a state of delirium, he would seize his revolver and shout: "Forward!"

And again the sleds would move northward. Stretching out his almost frozen hands in the sleeping bag, he would think with bitterness that the road ahead was much too long.

And what about the road back?

It seemed to him that all his life he had been mounting a steep staircase that did not always lead upward. Coming from the poorest strata, the son of a fisherman with a tumble-down farmstead on the Azov Sea, Sedov, by his very appearance in the world, was doomed to a gloomy and anonymous existence. But by his hard work and tremendous energy he succeeded in doing almost the impossible—he was promoted to the rank of Senior Lieutenant in the Navy, and obviously took pleasure in wearing the golden epaulets of an officer, thinking that they elevated him to the level of a first-class citizen. His merits in exploring the remote areas of Russia were duly marked by the Tsar, but the majority of Sedov's fellow officers, who had won their epaulets only by virtue of being blue bloods, openly despised him, and called him a "plebeian," an "upstart," almost to his face. He conceived the noblest of all deeds—bringing glory to his homeland by making a bold dash to the Pole. However, the organization of the expedition was entrusted to a newspaper sponsored by the Black Hundred—armed counterrevolutionaries. He embarked on his journey, fully determined to perform a great deed for the honor of his homeland. However, he had an old ship, untrained companions, weak dogs, and

34

dilapidated equipment. His contemporaries noted his happy-go-lucky, sociable disposition, but the sailors who began the journey with Sedov complained that he often threatened to shoot them if the sleds turned southward.

How tightly the noble and the evil had intertwined in the fate of one man.

A young officer has a burning passion for exploration and discoveries. He is honest. Inquisitive. Vulnerable. Bold. "Boldness on the verge of madness," noted one of his associates. In the majority of photographs of him that are extant, we see a daring seaman with a broad, open face. His bright eyes look straight ahead. A mustache and a goatee. The photographs radiate energy, strength, and a romantic soul.

He was born to become a trailblazer, to journey over ice, deserts, and mountains. He was lucky to be born at a time when there were still vast areas of terra incognita, and both Poles—North and South—were still a mystery.

How did Sedov himself explain his passion to reach the Pole? "I have no doubt whatever that having studied the Pole and the adjacent regions, we shall solve the greatest mystery of Nature. Who, if not those . . . who have settled the North, should reach the Pole? And I declare here and now: the Pole shall be conquered by Russians."

The fervent soul of Georgi Sedov could not reconcile itself to the fact that Russia lagged behind its northern neighbors in exploring the Arctic, and had not as yet participated in the race for the Pole.

After collecting a scanty sum for the voyage, and even that with great difficulty, he set sail for Novaya Zemlya in the summer of 1912, on board the vessel *St. Foka*. Of all the polar expeditions to date, this was surely the most pitiful. The merchants had supplied the ship with tainted salt pork and rotten cod. Instead of huskies, they had palmed off mongrels. The decrepit *St. Foka* developed a leak before it had even left the port at Archangel. The

Marine Ministry refused to provide the expedition a radio operator. The police insisted on documentary proof of the loyalty of the seamen who were hired. There was a catastrophic shortage of coal and warm clothing.

On February 15, 1914, after two very cold winters, scurvy, and hunger, the thirty-seven-year-old Georgi Sedov, accompanied by two sailors, set out from Tikhaya Bay on Franz Josef Land for the North Pole.

He was exhausted and gravely ill. His comrades tried to talk him out of making the trip. But Sedov was adamant.

"Is this the sort of equipment needed to reach the Pole? Was it with this outfit that I had counted on reaching it? Instead of eighty dogs, we have only twenty. And we ourselves are not as strong as we should be. None of them, of course, will stop us from doing our duty. We shall do our duty."

The roar of cannons. The yelping of dogs. Shouts of hurrah, together with the steam coming from a couple of dozen throats on that frosty day. That is how Lieutenant Georgi Sedov set out on his dash to the Pole.

"Goodbye, not farewell!"

Farewell, Lieutenant. Farewell.

March set in, but the cold would not let up; what is more, heavy blizzards struck hard. Sedov was in bad shape. He had a fever. His legs became swollen and were covered with horrible purple splotches. His heart was beating like mad. The pain almost split his head. He refused to take food and often slipped into a stupor. Probably there were moments when Sedov realized he would never make it to the Pole, but even at death's door he could not, would not, admit this.

"No, it's too early to give up. I must triumph over adversity," he would repeat, his teeth chattering, in his few relatively lucid moments.

The howling wind tore at the walls of the sailcloth tent as pellets of snow beat out a tattoo and the primus stove hummed with a blue flame. After cold shivers, Sedov was gripped by fever. For many days now, Sedov, fatally ill, had lain on a bed of sea ice, the hoarfrost his only blanket.

But never did he give the order to turn back.

He died on March 5, on a dark, blizzardy night. Seamen Linnik and Pustoshny buried Sedov on Rudolf Island, the last bit of Russian land on the way to the Pole. On his grave they laid the flag he had wanted to raise over the Pole.

Some say he might have avoided death, that it was the result of madness, a blind passion that blotted out all reason. (Two thousand kilometers on sleds drawn by weak dogs? they ask, eyebrows raised. Provisions for only one way?) But most of us, in our hearts at least, take another stand. "To die as Sedov died," a poet once wrote.

In May of 1937, heavy cargo planes took off from Rudolf Island, not far from the final resting place of Georgi Sedov. They were carrying to the North Pole the personnel of the world's first scientific drifting station, NP-1, the expedition of Ivan Papanin.

In August 1977, seamen from the atomic-powered icebreaker *Arktika*, the first surface vessel in the world to reach the Pole, raised the State Flag of the USSR on the top of the planet, symbolically attaching to it the staff of Sedov's flag.

Time and history do justice to real heroes and their exploits.

March 6. The last group arrives at Kotelny from Tiksi: chief of the expedition, Dmitri Shparo; a representative from headquarters, Oleg Obukhov; and cameramen and TV correspondents. Now that all of us are here, we can start setting up our base radio station. Two Caterpillar-type tractors with sleds and a snowmobile continue to haul our cargo from the Temp Bay airstrip to the RNS. And considering the bitter cold, this is not all that simple:

here metal crumbles like graphite; time and again the machines break down.

An argument about magnetic declinations comes up at lunchtime. Fyodor Sklokin claims that the magnetic pole is to the right of Kotelny, while Yuri Khmelevsky tries to prove it is to the left. Geographer Mikhail Deyev attempts to clear up the question: one should speak not of the magnetic pole, but of the magnetic meridian, and this meridian, in the region of the New Siberian Islands, makes some kind of tricky curve.

All this talk about compasses, theodolites, coordinates, and declinations is quite understandable. The question of pinpointing the skiing group's whereabouts is of vital importance. In the absence of any landmarks, they will have to determine their position using only the celestial bodies. And what if the sky is hidden by clouds, or the theodolite is damaged? What if the chronometers stop? In this unforgiving environment, nothing can be left to chance.

This is why Yuri Khmelevsky and Vladimir Rakhmanov are busy day and night—testing their instruments, examining tables, studying maps of magnetic declinations. They have brought several theodolites with them, each of a somewhat different design; all of them will undergo rigorous tests, and only the "winners" will have the right to continue the journey. Already some of these instruments have failed the test of the Arctic cold. Our sextants too must pass these shakedown tests: the requirements set by Khmelevsky boil down to the following: it must be possible to see a star through the eyepiece in the daytime. The weight and dependability of the theodolites are compared, as is their ability to stand up to wear and tear along the way.

Our navigators also prepare the chronometers for the skiing group. To know the exact time during the journey is a must. To determine coordinates, one of the navigators, using the theodolite, must note the height of the sun while another fixes this moment on the chronometer; then the observations are processed with the help of specially prepared tables, and in the evening the radio operator is given a sheet of paper with the exact coordinates.

Khmelevsky takes special care with the skiiers' timepieces. He has had soft cases made for the six marine chronometers (these give the time with an accuracy of up to two-tenths of a second) and has forbidden the men to wear their electronic watches on their wrists. He has ordered them instead to sew the watches inside the breast pockets of their shirts. "This way we're killing two birds with one stone," explained Yuri. "We're keeping the watches warm and protecting them from shock at the same time."

March 7. This morning bad news swept across the station: the mechanic had disappeared. Everyone gathered around Misha, the local inhabitant who drives the cross-country vehicle. He is a good-natured, bearded fellow.

"Darn it," he moans, "the mechanic has disappeared."

"What do you mean 'disappeared'? How come? Speak up!"

"If I only knew where." He shrugged his shoulders sorrowfully. "He went into the tundra and did not return."

"Then what are you standing here for? This is ridiculous! Let's organize a search party. Why don't you warm up the snowmobile?"

Misha seemed a bit dazed by this response. He looked at us as if we were planning to go to the moon rather than the Pole. Then someone asked a question more to the point.

"What does he look like?"

"He was pretty small and had red hair."

"Red hair? I don't seem to remember him."

"Don't remember him?" exclaimed Misha, a bit offended. "In the daytime you couldn't chase him out of the diesel room, and at night he would always sleep in the hallway. He would curl himself up like a doughnut and sleep on the floor right in the doorway. He was great when it came to eating—always begging for sugar, remember? And if he ever was given a bone, he would polish it so that it glistened."

At last we caught on: "Mechanic" is the name of Misha's little puppy. Now about three months old, he was born in the fierce cold of winter and grew up in the warm diesel room. That's how he got his name.

You can understand that no one went into the tundra looking for the dog. We expressed our sympathy to Misha and went back to our work. Sklokin summoned the team to set up the antenna system. In a small hut some one hundred meters from the main building, Labutin continued to assemble and tune a powerful receiver-transmitter that would keep us in direct touch with Moscow. While Khmelevsky and Davydov were packing our daily rations for the trek, Melnikov was getting the batteries ready. The rest were unpacking crates, pulling cables, checking the equipment—in short, everyone was busy.

That evening the team with its skis and rucksacks boarded the sled, and Misha, at the controls of his snowmobile, drove up to the ice shelf at the request of the TV cameramen in order to simulate the group's start for the Pole. The TV people had no time to wait for the real start and so had decided to stage a departure. We had barely left the RNS when the snowmobile came to a sudden halt. Misha jumped out of the cab and headed into the tundra. Rolling down the hill toward him was some kind of creature—a wolf? a polar fox?

"It's Mechanic!" someone shouted, and so it was. Misha took the pup in his arms, climbed back into the cab, and off we went again.

40

On the ice just off the shore, the men of the ski team put on their skis, strapped on their rucksacks, and began accommodating the cameramen. This was real torture. The mercury had dipped below minus forty degrees centigrade, causing white blisters to puff up on their faces, requiring continuous rubbing with wool mittens. Because of the cold, the movie camera regularly got stuck, and the film in it crumbled like mica. Finally the cameraman, who could hardly breathe the air it was so cold, announced that because the sun was setting they would stop filming for the day. Everyone heaved a sigh of relief.

This first outing on skis, though it might seem frivolous, was nevertheless very important for the skiers. At last they could remember, and feel again on their own skin, the cold of a real frost, the real conditions of a skiing expedition. The cold was merciless, it was everywhere—it was a killer frost. Here was the first serious obstacle on the way to the Pole. Until this moment there had been only talk about the journey, but today the first ski tracks were left on the Arctic ice.

Upon returning to the RNS, all of us seemed a bit stunned at first. For a while we just sat there. And then all at once came an outpouring of remarks.

"We must dress more warmly."

"Those gloves might be called Arktika but they should be called Africa."

"The down mittens are no good at all. Only fur is warm in cold like this."

"The ski poles freeze your hands."

The one who seemed most concerned was Khmelevsky, who was virtually made blind by the frost: the steam of his breath had instantly coated his glasses with ice. Time and again he was forced to stop, unfasten his ski poles, take off his mittens, wipe his glasses. In the meantime the tip of his nose would become white and brittle, so he would have to warm his face. Then his glasses would ice up again, and so on and on.

In the evening Dmitri and I sat down to do an update. I showed him a radiogram that said the airstrip on Zhokhov Island, which we were to use as a steppingstone to our jumping-off point, would probably not be ready to receive aircraft for another ten days.

"That's bad news." Dmitri went over the message again. "Maybe we should not hurry with the start," he said. "We could start out later."

I was dumbfounded. Until this moment, all of Shparo's efforts were aimed only at bringing the start as soon as possible.

"The cold," I made a guess. "It worries you?"

In silence, he nodded his head.

"But these temperatures may last until April. We are in Yakutia, and this is the Arctic."

"I know," agreed Dmitri. "Of course, we'll start just as soon as we're ready, without delay. I really did not mean it."

We continued discussing other matters but finally returned to the subject of the cold.

"Probably this severe cold oppresses me more than the others," Shparo admitted. "My fingers and face were frostbitten on previous expeditions, so the skin in those places is very vulnerable now. It's difficult not to think about it."

He remained silent for a moment, and then in a firm voice announced: "But in all ticklish situations, I always relied on my experience. On Taimyr once it was much colder, and we survived."

March 9. It's nice and cozy behind the steel walls of the RNS that separate us from the Arctic. It's bright and warm. Modern furnishings. But the main thing is the feeling of comradeship. I believe that the most horrible thing in the North is to be alone. It is not the cold, not the polar night, not the ice nor the blizzards, but loneliness—that is man's main enemy in the Arctic.

Our base station is changing before our very eyes. On both sides of the building the antenna system has gone up: the masts have been raised and the sky is criss-crossed by wires. The main receiver-transmitter is operating at full capacity. When all this equipment came to life, when the lamps lit up and started buzzing, our senior radio operator, Labutin, usually a very reserved man about fifty years old, was so overjoyed that he started singing in a loud voice. Then almost at once he seemed to forget everyone in the room, shutting himself off from his immediate surround by donning his earphones and floating off into the airwaves. I hardly ever see him at lunch or supper, and I have my doubts as to whether he even returns to his bunk to sleep.

At about seven in the morning, the ski team with all their equipment went out onto the ice of the lagoon. Ledenev and Shishkarev set up a tent and lit the primus stove. Inside the tent it was simply wonderful. I climbed into a sleeping bag that was lying right on the snow.

I wanted to be accepted as "one of the boys" in the tent. I wanted to set out with them across the ice like we used to. In the evenings, with a sense of duty fulfilled, to gather together in the tent, to slip into a down sleeping bag, to sip hot tea, to warm your hands around the plate of food, and to immerse ourselves in a state of bliss, tranquillity and warmth, slowly but surely sailing away into the Land of Nod.

Those moments in the tent were always the happiest for me.

But now it was time to return to the RNS for breakfast. As we emerged from the tent, we were surprised to see that everything had changed. Just ten minutes ago there had been no wind at all, the temperature a relatively mild minus thirty-five. But now all this had been changed as if by the wave of a magic wand: the sudden onset of a blizzard blotted out all landmarks, even the buildings of

43

the nearby polar station and the slopes of the shore. The wind was howling in a vicious but even tempo, driving an endless wave of snow along the ground. The view, of course, was breathtaking, and it was at that moment that I felt I was really back in the Arctic. It was precisely such a blizzard and concomitant ground wind that was my first encounter with the Far North, precisely this kind of weather—the sun shining dimly through a shroud of snow, the wind driving wave after wave of snow along the endless horizon. Meanwhile the blizzard was gaining momentum every minute. It was a bone-chilling cold, but even so we felt a moment of joy—the wind seemed to awaken some latent energy in us, something new, powerful, tingling. Here we were, at last, face to face with the real North! That is when everything inside you seems to sing out: we must keep on struggling and win! Leaving our tent on the lagoon, we headed for home. As we climbed up the slope of the shore, I looked behind me and beheld a truly majestic sight: reflecting the tender gold of the sun, braid after braid of the wind-driven snow seemed to intertwine, forming incredible patterns. The outlines of the men walking behind me resembled figures in a watercolor while in the distance, between gusts of the blizzard, I could make out the silhouette of the lonely orange tent.

The hero of the day was Vladimir Rakhmanov. When an important wire in the antenna became entangled at a height of twenty meters, Rakhmanov, without uttering a word, climbed up the guywire. The vicious cold and gale force winds made life even on the ground very miserable. Imagine, then, what it was like for our comrade, who for about an hour hung by a hawser between sky and earth. Rahkmanov amazed everyone with this feat. At our evening briefing session, at which we summed up the work of the day and handed out tomorrow's assignments, I presented Vladimir a special award "For the Will To Win."

He was rather embarrassed by it all, even blushing when we gave him a round of applause.

March 10. The hydrometeorological observatory at Tiksi regularly supplies us with forecasts of the weather along our route. Today, to the north of Henrietta Island it was to be clear, cold, and still. But here on Kotelny a snowstorm was raging full blast. The wind, seemingly gone berserk, lashed at the snow, raising clouds of white crystals so thick you could see only a few meters in front of you.

Here is a paradox: this morning everyone went out into that hellish weather more enthusiastically than they had yesterday, when it was milder, and then with a special furor they worked on the rigging of the antenna despite the raging blizzard. Dmitri, who often walks around with an anxious and displeased look on his face, today found no reason whatsoever to rebuke his colleagues.

The conclusion is obvious: the greater the fury of the Arctic, the greater the willpower of each of us.

The fate of Vasili Shishkarev was finally decided today. He was given a berth on the team heading for the Pole, although it was not without considerable hesitation that Dmitri took this step. Just a few days before leaving Moscow, the sports medicine specialists who kept tabs on the health of the expedition members asked Vasili to undergo a more thorough checkup. There was something about his heart that made them somewhat wary. Accompanied by Vadim Davydov, Vasili set out for the hospital, and in the evening handed us a medical report. Swiftly glancing through the bulk of the report, filled with many unknown terms, I slowly read and reread the conclusion: "Participation in a long and arduous trek to the North Pole is contraindicated." I was afraid to look up. For Vasili the recommendation must have been like a terrible punch below the belt, and I thought that at any moment he might be unable to control his emotions.

45

But much to my surprise, Vasili was quite calm. His narrow, deep-set eyes looked straight ahead as always, and with just a bit of mockery in them.

"Don't let it get you down, Vasili. You'll work with the group at the base camp."

"It hasn't got me down," he replied, in an even voice. "I'll make it to the Pole myself, without you."

"What do you mean?"

"I'll go alone. Later. I'll prove it to all of you."

By that time I had gotten to know Vasili well enough not to simply shrug off his words as a silly joke. Let me tell you about him.

Vasili has the build of a real athlete. Clothes cannot conceal his rippling muscles. His lean face, high cheekbones, and narrow eyes make him look a bit like a Tatar. With people he does not know well he is overmodest and even reserved. With his friends, however, he is fond of arguing a point, and will uphold his own view to the bitter end, a view which, as a rule, has nothing in common with the opinions of others, no matter what authority their names might carry. He works as a gardener for a regional road building and city planning department. He writes poetry.

At the beginning of the seventies, when we first tried skiing over drifting ice, Vasili was living in the small town of Lepsy, in Kazakhstan. He did not miss a single newspaper item about our treks and plans. In 1973 he wrote a letter to *Komsomolskaya Pravda,* saying: "I have learned that an expedition is preparing to go to the Pole, and I ask to be included on the team. My professional training was as an electrician. I have made several long distance journeys across Kazakhstan by bicycle, on skis, and on foot."

At that time, of course, we were receiving many letters like that. In a most courteous manner, Dmitri replied, as he did to all such letters: the team for the expedition

46

has already been picked, and in general you live pretty far from Moscow. Wishing you all the best, etc.

No one could imagine that some young man living four thousand kilometers from Moscow could be considered for the expedition. By that time we already had a very close-knit team, on which everyone knew his duties, and the members of which were linked to each other not only by the bonds of their common cause, but also by a real spirit of camaraderie. We were always together at our training sessions, and we were always together on holidays.

Unlike others "knocking at the door" of our expedition, Vasili did not give up when he was turned down. Over the next two years we received regular letters from him. "Could you please send a schedule of your training sessions?" he asked in one letter. "I've begun training by myself," he reported in another. Finally we decided that the man had only one chance of making our team: he had to prove to us that he was absolutely necessary to the expedition. Brooking no delay, he got down to business. In a ringing frost, Vasili, all alone, crossed the ice of Lake Balkhash. This two hundred kilometer trek of his raised our eyebrows and made us consider him in a different light. For two winters in a row he did not live in his house; instead he set up a tent in his backyard, made himself a sleeping bag, and, to the amazement of his townsmen, overcoming the snickering of neighbors and the grumbling of his mother, accustomed himself to the cold.

"When I first heard about the expedition to the Pole," Vasili told me later on, "I really felt as if I were bewitched. I once read a newspaper article about a young man who was training to be a cosmonaut, but he perished tragically just before his dream of traveling into space came true. Man can do anything! That was the main idea of the newspaper article. And for me, it became my credo."

For six long years he kept trying to prove that the

expedition needed him. At Dmitri's suggestion, he moved to Moscow in 1976. At our training sessions he always ran farther than the others, always chose the heaviest barbell. During our summer journeys around Taimyr Peninsula he always asked for the toughest of jobs. He fathomed the mysteries of getting his bearings by the stars, and thereby became a backup navigator. He learned to operate our transmitter, and became a backup radio operator. He performed all the jobs involved in preparing our equipment, and could therefore stand in for our quartermaster. The main thing, however, was that he became our trusted comrade and faithful companion on the road to the Pole.

We became accustomed to his thorny character, and also to the fact that Vasili has his own point of view on absolutely everything. The only thing we could not reconcile ourselves to was that our new comrade, who was young, energetic, and bright, had no desire to further his education. His job as a gardener (mowing lawns, planting trees, trimming shrubs) suited him quite nicely. In response to all our rebukes, Vasili, in an offended tone of voice, came up with a reply which was obviously not what he had on his mind. The gist of his answer was approximately the following: "Why should I graduate from your institute when I earn no less than an engineer anyway?" Or the following: "Someone has to dig the earth and plant flowers." But more often than not, Vasili simply felt offended and would leave the room; there was no sense in discussing the subject any further.

And it was only here, on Kotelny Island, that I found out the truth behind his seeming lack of ambition. One evening, in a moment of frankness, Vasili told me that he dreamed of studying at a literature institute, that he was seriously thinking of becoming a poet. I did not know what to say to that. As I see it, writing good poetry is much more difficult than conquering the North Pole. Incidentally, Vasili had already proven once that man can do anything.

Not once did he express his desire for a berth on the ski team that was to go to the Pole. However, when it came to actually selecting the team, it became clear that Shishkarev's participation was sort of tacitly understood, and that no one had any doubts whatsoever on that account.

And then, all of a sudden, that medical report. . . .

Vasili himself stubbornly claimed that he was absolutely in good health, and that he would go to the Pole anyway—if not with us, then by himself.

Dmitri was tormented by the decision. On the one hand, he had faith in Vasili's dependability and strength of character, while on the other, he could not doubt the competence of the doctors who said no. Who was to be the seventh man? The tent was made for seven men; all the rations had been packed for seven members. There were two substitutes—Shatokhin and Deyev—who was it going to be? From Tiksi, Dmitri placed a call to Moscow, to the Institute of Medico-Biological Research, whose scientific program the expedition had been carrying out since 1971. At the other end of the line was our old friend, Mikhail Novikov, chief of the Psychology Laboratory.

"Shishkarev?" he asked again, and after a short pause, he replied quite firmly: "My considered opinion is that Vasili is able to go to the Pole."

You have to know Dmitri: as always, he wanted to be one hundred percent sure. He did not want to take any chances with Vasili's health, and he did not want to take any chances with the success of the ski team. He realized full well what a wrong decision could lead to. His doubts continued to torment him.

Yesterday evening, Shparo, Khmelevsky, and Davydov met for a "consultation" on the matter.

"The diagnosis is serious," said Davydov. "High blood pressure. Yet the details in the medical report actually nullify all our apprehensions."

"But what about the conclusion?" Shparo asked, a note of gloom in his voice: " 'Participation in a long and arduous trek to the North Pole is contraindicated.' Hmm. 'Contraindicated.' " And then he seemed to brighten somewhat. "For me," he mused, "radiculitis contraindicates my carrying a rucksack, but only when I am under a heavy rucksack do I feel really well."

"You know, Dmitri," said Davydov, "I've weighed all the pros and cons, and I vote that Vasili can go to the Pole."

"How about you?" Shparo turned to Khmelevsky.

Yuri was not so categorical as Davydov, but the essence of his reply was that Shishkarev be given a berth on the team.

"Perhaps the results of the checkup were due to the fact that during the past three weeks Vasili had practically no rest at all," he surmised. "I'm not sure he had any sleep at all during that time."

"Yes," Dmitri agreed. "We all had it pretty tough then, but in the evenings each of us went home, had some rest and relaxation with our families. But in his bachelor's dormitory, Vasili was without rest and without the warmth of family surroundings. Even his appearance has changed—he has grown pallid, and looks older."

The final confab was held today.

"Do you realize that your participation jeopardizes not only your own life, but also the outcome of the cause to which we have dedicated many years of our lives?"

Shparo had begun with none of the usual diplomatic niceties, looking Vasili directly in the face.

Shishkarev returned his stare.

"I'm sure I won't let you down," replied Vasili. "I have never in my whole life experienced any hardships due to my health. You yourself know that I am stronger and have more stamina than anyone."

"That I know," agreed Dmitri. "But I hope you understand why I want to exclude the slightest risk."

"I won't let you down."

Vasili could offer no further arguments.

With just a little more hesitation, Dmitri gave his consent.

Everything was back in place.

March 11. Our work at base camp is just about done. The pilots have sent a radiogram indicating they will fly the expedition to the jumping-off point on March 14. But the blizzard is still blowing hard and strong, and the temperature hovers around minus thirty. Many of our party already show traces of frostbite on their faces.

Nothing extraordinary has occurred today except that Oleg Obukhov has invited a pretty radio operator from the neighboring polar station, and this, quite naturally, has caused a stir in our strictly male community.

According to the evening forecast, the weather tomorrow will be unchanged: strong winds, snow, and continued cold.

March 12. Today is bath day. The fire in the stove of the small wooden bathhouse, some fifty meters from the RNS, has been burning since morning. It is not so simple to get the temperature of the steam up to the necessary level in this windblown bathhouse. We got our water by melting chunks of ice we had prepared the day before.

The first to go into the steam were the hosts of the station; after supper, it was our turn. The blizzard was so thick that we virtually had to grope our way to the bathhouse. My turn in the steamroom was with Vadim—an expert in steambaths, a real professor on the subject of Russian bathhouses.

In the dressing room the floor beneath the wooden frames was covered with a thick layer of ice. The wind blew snow through cracks in the walls. Yet the steamroom welcomed us with warmth and, once Vadim stoked the fire, it even became hot. The five of us climbed to the top shelf and were in a state of bliss until the same Vadim ordered us to come down, saying that it was useless to waste time, and that we should get down to the real business. He threw several dippers of water on the scorching hot stones, and the room became filled with hardly bearable, yet strangely blissful steam. Then he ordered Dmitri to lie down on the top shelf and began to flog him with a bundle of birch twigs brought from Moscow especially for this purpose. And Dmitri simply moaned from pleasure. In the same manner Davydov flogged all the others, after which, with red and tingling bodies, and birch leaves stuck to us here and there, we ran in the nude out into the blizzard to cool off, instead of taking the usual dip in a cold swimming pool, as we did back in Moscow.

Ledenev by that time had almost finished dressing, but witnessing this scene, he undressed once again and went to the top shelf of the steamroom to "get down to the real business."

After our bath we drank hot tea, argued most fervently about the church and religion, about the influence of love on creativity, and about the upbringing of children.

March 13. Tomorrow we fly out to our jumping-off point. This morning we received a radiogram from Victor Krivosheya, senior navigator of the Kolyma-Indigir Air Detachment: "On March 14 we plan to fly the ski team from the Kotelny Island polar station on board two AN-2s to Zhokhov Island. From Zhokhov to Henrietta Island the group will be airlifted by an MI-8 helicopter, which will also allow for ice reconnaissance in the starting area. Sklokin's base camp group will be flown to NP-24 by IL-14 according to schedule."

For the entire day, talk has centered around this communication. Actually, everyone was expecting it, and we knew that sooner or later our preparations must have an end. The mood of the group changed instantly; in place of the businesslike hustle and bustle prevailing a few moments earlier, a solemn mood settled over us, though this was not devoid of an intense inner excitement.

Late this evening, the whole expedition met in our cozy little dining room. It was an informal but almost ceremonious gathering, a very special and affecting kind of send-off. We all sat shoulder to shoulder around the table as Shparo began to speak.

"We start tomorrow," he began. "Yet I do not wish to speak about the adventure or the thrill of reaching the Pole, but about those of us who are staying behind to work at our support bases.

"Leonid Labutin is a man dedicated to our cause. He began training for the trek to the Pole in 1973 and since then has put all his energy into the expedition. Chronologically, Leonid is older than any of us, but in spirit he is younger than many. I would like to remind all of you that Labutin developed the radio communications system for the expedition, and he also designed the unique 'Ledovaya' radio station for the ski team. Leonid Labutin is to be my deputy and, at the same time, chief of the base-camp radio station here on Kotelny.

"Fyodor Sklokin is appointed chief of the group at NP-24. For me, he is more than just the athletic trainer of the expedition; he is actually the eighth member of the ski team. Fyodor, you will have to tackle a wide range of problems by yourself, such as supplies for the ski team, its safety, radio communications, and in general, right from the beginning, you will have to take all the responsibility on yourself. I've known you for eight years, and I am confident you will be able to meet the challenge.

"Special mention must be made of the stand-ins for the ski team. Mikhail Deyev, the substitute navigator, will stay with Labutin on Kotelny, and Alexander Shatokhin, the substitute radio operator, will be based at NP-24. Both men have an ardent desire to accompany us to the Pole, and both are indeed quite worthy to go. Although you remain at your respective bases, you must be ready, if need be, to take the place of any member of the ski team.

"Another radio operator who will be working at NP-24 is Georgi Ivanov, whose dedication and enthusiasm must be applauded.

"And I promise you, my friends, that at the Pole we shall be all together—this is my second wish after that of conquering the Pole. For many years now, we have all been marching toward this goal, and our victory will be shared by all."

With this, Dmitri produced a bottle of buckthorn liqueur and poured it out evenly among the whole group, each one having but a few golden drops at the bottom of his glass. "I propose a round of toasts going clockwise. Fyodor, you lead the parade!"

Sklokin: "For the sake of the expedition we have all sacrificed a great deal. We might have advanced our careers instead, or have spent more time with our families. But has anyone ever tried to estimate what these years of dedication have given us? We have learned the meaning of true comradeship, and have blended together into a close-knit team. Each of us knows that he has true friends here. And you are absolutely right, Dmitri, in saying that marching to the Pole there will be not seven of us, but the whole group—every one of us! And so I raise my glass for a good start!"

Ivanov: "Our radio will be a bridge keeping you in touch with the mainland and inspiring you with confidence. We won't let you down. Good luck!"

Davydov: "In 1976, when we returned from our training expedition from NP-23, I made an astounding discovery for myself: hundreds, thousands, tens of thousands of people wanted to meet us, to look at us, to speak to us about our journey, to get our autographs. After that, I realized very clearly that our expedition does not concern our little group alone, but that each of us has a great duty to millions of other people. During our preparations for this trek to the Pole, we realized this especially clearly.

Everyone, from government ministers to skilled crafts-men, found time to help us, to give us assistance in pre-paring the necessary equipment. I think I can say that each and every one of us experiences a profound feeling of responsibility to these people, to those who had faith in the expedition and helped it. And my toast is to the good health of all!"

Deyev: "The only thing I have left to say is: to our meeting where all the meridians come to a point."

Rakhmanov: "All right, guys, let's not miss this chance!"

Melnikov: "What is the real meaning behind skiing to the Pole? It means that we can do it, that we are strong. This is a most serious undertaking. And our feeling of responsibility to our native land will help us reach this goal. One other thing. For many years now we have been celebrating holidays together. And together we sweated it out at our training sessions. But now the arrangements for our expedition will separate us for almost three months: the ski team will move northward over the ice fields, the radio operators will take up their positions at their respective bases. But our hearts will beat in unison. Each of us will give his all for the common victory. And I raise this toast to those who are waiting for us back home, for those who have faith in us."

Shatokhin: "Earlier this year a rock fell on me from out of the blue. I suspect it was part of a meteorite, a piece of some star. That star has cooled off, has smashed itself to smithereens, yet we shall continue to burn forever, to be a monolith to the end!"

Shishkarev: "There are not so many Poles left in our lives. I drink to those who were in the expedition and are not now with us, and to those who are in it now—to our whole wonderful team!"

Ledenev: "No matter what the public response to the expedition, I am certain that the days spent here will be the best days of our lives. We have traveled a long and difficult road to our jumping-off point on Henrietta Island, and we were guided along this road by our faith in victory. And it is a very good thing indeed that we have retained this faith. Because now it will be much more difficult than before. We have prepared well for our future trials, both physically and with respect to our equipment. I would like now to propose a toast to tactfulness, to mutual understanding, and to love."

Khmelevsky: "I am happy we have lived to see this day. I would like to propose a toast to fulfillment of each of our dreams. But dreams do not come true by themselves—it requires stout hearts, faith in one's idea, friendship, and sometimes the ability to put more trust in your comrades than in yourself. And so, to all that has shown itself in our struggle for the North Pole, do I raise this glass!"

Shparo: "My heart is really thumping—I've never been so excited. I know we shall do our duty."

As we emptied our glasses of those few golden drops, our faces radiated willpower, confidence, and an extraordinary elation.

March 14. Our meeting lasted long past midnight. Afterward I sat in the dining room at my typewriter, preparing the morning's dispatch. Khmelevsky, Ledenev, and Deyev had stayed up to do the dishes; obviously they wanted this wonderful evening to continue, and to speak what was in their hearts.

"Did you notice the happiness, the intense feeling of closeness among us, the group cohesion?" Yuri asked me. "Stress that in your write-up so that everyone gets the message: be as strongly united and as purposeful as the men who are heading for the North Pole."

I pounded my typewriter till four in the morning and went to bed. At eight, Shparo shook my shoulder. "Contact Temp Bay and find out whether the planes are planning to pick us up."

In his heart, Dmitri probably hoped for another day to get ready, that due to bad weather the flights today would be canceled. I switched on the radio next to my bed, and immediately heard the voice of the operator at Temp Bay: "We have no plans for flying out today."

That could mean only one thing: no aircraft should be expected within the next couple of days.

Dmitri heaved a sigh of relief, but that very instant, and over the same frequency, we heard the voice of an operator about a kilometer away from our polar station. He said quite confidently that according to information he had received, the planes had already taken off and were headed our way. What were we to believe? I shrugged my shoulders and switched off the radio. Shparo sighed even more deeply, slammed his fist into his hand, and said: "We've got to get ready."

Quickly splashing my face with water, I hustled over to the station to teletype my article to Moscow. We had to hurry: if the planes were really on their way, then our hours on Kotelny were numbered. Crossing the lagoon, I climbed the steep shore to the cluster of one-storied wooden buildings and immediately saw the chief of the station—the huge, black-bearded Azerbaijanian, Alik Kaziev. He stood by one of the buildings, hatless, his sheepskin coat unbuttoned, revealing a thin nylon shirt underneath. This Southerner, it seemed, was absolutely insensitive to the cold. My unprotected face was aching from the cold, but Kaziev, as if molded of another clay, felt quite at ease standing there half dressed in the razorsharp wind.

No matter what he was occupied with—his job, hunting, receiving guests, or looking after his young son—Kasiev always seemed gloomy, even hostile, although at heart he was kindly and mild-mannered. "Look what the dogs are doing," he said, shaking my hand. "That's how they feel the blizzard."

Following me were three huge huskies. They had just been romping around, playfully snapping at each other, but now—and it was true—they looked as if bewitched: they rolled around in the snow on their backs, pawing the air.

"That's the truest barometer," mumbled Kaziev. "Even though the sky is clear this moment, it soon won't be."

We entered the radio room, where I handed my article to the operators, and stepped back outside to return to camp. I was dumbfounded. The blizzard was howling, the wind shrieking like a banshee in the antenna, and there was snow everywhere.

"Well, that's it," said Kaziev, even more gloomily than usual. "You're not flying out today."

I could hardly make headway against the wind, but finally made it to the lagoon. Almost immediately I heard the roar of engines, and in a few minutes saw two small twin-engine planes anxiously circling overhead, above the wild blizzard. It was clear the pilots could not make out the polar station, the RNS, nor the lagoon where they could make a landing.

Were they really going to risk it? The last thing we needed was a plane crash. Twice I fired rockets into the air, but instead of recognizing them as danger signals the pilots took them as landing-strip markers. It was a good thing I was standing on the lagoon and not on the knoll! Judging by the sound of their engines, the aircraft had revved down. I could hardly believe my eyes: floating just a bit above the knoll, amid a fountain of snow, came first one plane and then the other, fighting their way against the wind. All of a sudden, my heart skipped a beat: what if the pilots failed to see the slope and came down too early? But their calculations were flawless. The AN-2S—"Annies" we call them—touched down like helicopters: facing a strong headwind, they seemed to hover without motion above the lagoon, then slapped down with their skis onto the ice, skidded forward for about thirty meters, and came to a standstill.

I dashed toward the aircraft. People who had witnessed the scene from the polar station were also running down to the lagoon. By the time we arrived, the pilots were standing beside their planes like actors from some benefit performance. Though they were not taking their bows, I could sense they really appreciated our sincere expressions of admiration. Personally, I had never seen anything like this, not even in the movies.

The crews were taken to have lunch, and we busied ourselves getting ready for the takeoff. It always happens this way when you wait for something an especially long time: you wait and prepare for the moment, and then it comes and catches you off guard. Two hours to takeoff.

As is customary in Russia before setting out on a long journey, we all gathered together; those about to depart, the base camp crew, and our hosts assembled in the polar station's tiny wardroom. As is also the custom, no one said a word. Everyone felt a bit sad, of that I am sure. It was a touching farewell. The women (the cooks, the station chief's wife) even shed some tears.

As we were loading the aircraft, the blizzard quieted down just as suddenly as it had appeared. The wind let up; visibility was good. At two in the afternoon, the Annies took off and headed for Zhokhov Island. Aboard the two planes were the seven members of the ski team, three cameramen, photographer Sasha Abazha, Oleg Obukhov, and myself.

It was a long flight. Because of the crates and rucksacks, it was very crowded in the planes, and what is more, it was cold. Due to the awkward positions we were forced to assume (some sat on the floor or on crates, while others sat on each other's laps), all of us developed cramps in our legs. It was very dark by the time we finally landed.

Night and bitter cold reigned on the Zhokhov Island, a tiny bit of terra firma in the Arctic Ocean. From here to our jumping-off point it was still two hundred kilometers, but the planes could fly us no further, since on Henrietta Island there is no place to land. In the morning we would board a helicopter for the last leg.

March 15. We spent the night on Zhokhov in a tractor-drawn house-trailer on runners, planning to fly further the next day. Early that morning, as we emerged from the trailer, we were struck by the beauty of an unusual scene: to the right, above a snow-covered knoll hung a huge, bright moon, the kind you can see only in the Arctic, while to the left, slowly rising, was a reddish-orange sun, just as big, but slightly flattened at the top, a sun that was alive . . . but cold. The air was pure and tingling, hoar-frost sparkling in the sky.

Before takeoff, we sat down for a few minutes with Victor Krivosheya, the man responsible for airlifting the group to its jumping-off point. We had to chart a plan for ice reconnaissance of the region north of Henrietta, to a distance of fifty kilometers.

At eight o'clock the helicopter easily lifted our whole group and its belongings, and took a northeasterly course. Now only an hour's flight separated us from that cherished bit of land, Henrietta Island. But very soon this sweet hour would be only another memory. Everyone was excited, smiling as if we had already conquered the Pole.

It was planned that the helicopter would land the ski team and the accompanying party on the island and then, with the navigators of the expedition, would reconnoiter the nearby area. The ski team would start out, with the cameramen and photographers recording the moment for posterity, after which the helicopter would return the accompanying party to the mainland. Obukhov and I had the duty of officially recording the expedition's start for the North Pole.

When we finally caught sight of our destination, however, we had to radically alter our plans.

"Henrietta below us!" shouted Victor Krivosheya, sticking his head out of the pilot's cabin.

Everyone pressed their faces against the portholes. So that's what our cherished little island looked like. From the air it resembled a solitary sore tooth, a ragged cliff, jutting out of the frozen ocean. On three sides the island consisted of sheer granite cliffs; only the northern coast, though quite high, wasn't so rocky. Here we could make out the buildings of a long-deserted polar station. And right smack in the middle of the island loomed a big glacier shaped like half an eggshell.

But we could hardly have imagined what was happening around the island. I must confess I was a bit naive to have thought that Henrietta was "soldered" into a solid ice field, and that it would be no problem at all for our skiers to slip off the land onto the drifting ice. But directly off the island's southern face, thick water vapor rose from a patch of open water, while to the north and northwest its shores were swept by a broad current of sludge ice interspersed with large chunks and even whole icebergs.

Our smiles disappeared as if by magic.

The helicopter made several passes over the deserted station, and then touched down some fifty meters from it. Just then we saw a polar bear running down the rocky slope away from the buildings.

"I made several passes over the station just to scare him out," said Krivosheya. "That bear has been living here for years."

We unloaded our gear and together walked to the edge of the cliff. The view that unfolded was even more majestic than what we had seen from the air. Now we not only saw, we *heard*, the living ice below: from the heaving and thrashing current of ice we could hear crunching, groaning, rasping, crashing, and cracking sounds, as well as others for which we had no vocabulary at all. The ice chunks collided, smashing themselves to smithereens, overturning, piling atop one another in a furious maelstrom.

"You won't find a better model for a painting entitled 'The End of the World,' " Rakhmanov mused.

To that there was no response. Oblivious to the cold, everyone seemed hypnotized by the scene before us. Finally it was Dmitri who shook us out of our trance.

"Khmelevsky, Rakhmanov, and myself," he barked, "are going to fly out for reconnaissance. The rest get down to work and pitch camp. Ledenev, you find out whether we can take up quarters in the house. Vadim, you see what you can do to get a fire going in the furnace."

To our great surprise and satisfaction, the relatively large house, which at one time had served as a base for those wintering here, proved to be in quite good condition. With our shovels we quickly cleared away the snowdrifts that covered the door right up to the roof line, and then, with crowbar and pickax, freed the entrance of ice. Inside, the building looked as if it had last been inhabited the past autumn and not a full twenty years ago. The windowpanes were intact; aluminum plates and saucers stood on the shelves. And there were many books. From the storeroom Vadim and Oleg brought coal and stoked up the stoves—first the one used for cooking, then a second one, quite tall, that was positioned so that it heated three rooms. The stoves burned nicely, but there was so much smoke that the house soon became quite murky. No doubt the chimneys had become clogged with ice.

Half an hour later, the helicopter returned from ice reconnaissance. There was nothing consoling that Dmitri could tell us. Our start would definitely be put off until the next morning. The helicopter, the cameramen on board, sallied upward and took a course for Zhokhov Island.

Treacherous Henrietta

Everyone was busy setting up house and inspecting the surviving structures of the polar station. Everyone except Shparo, that is. He just stood there, his back to the entrance of the main building, staring out at the floating ice, trying to fathom whether mere mortals could overcome this obstacle; trying to calculate the risk. As always in such crucial moments, he turned almost sullen, and fumbled for words when questions were addressed his way.

"You know what?" Dmitri turned to me, "this is exactly how I imagined Henrietta. Cliffs . . . a glacier . . . a sheer madness of ice pressing up against the land."

"You have a rich imagination," I grinned. "You know, of course, we're virtual prisoners here. It's impossible to leave the island on skis."

Dmitri did not object, but I knew that deep down he wanted to. The word *impossible* does not sit easy with him.

"Let's go down to the shore," he offered, "and get a closer look at the enemy."

From a nail driven into the wall near the door, I grabbed a ten-round carbine and slipped it over my shoulder. Dmitri loaded his mini-mortar, a rocket pistol the size of a fountain pen, which is part of the standard rescue kit for pilots and cosmonauts. These precautions were not overkill; the polar bear we had flushed out of the station was still wandering around here somewhere. Judging from the size of his footprints—and there were plenty of them around—the beast was a splendid specimen. An encounter with him could hold nothing good in store. In all likelihood he was rather disgruntled by our unceremonious intrusion, and all our previous contacts with these masters of the Arctic had taught us to be cautious and respectful toward them, to give them as wide a berth as possible.

As we descended the steep incline to the shore, we saw more bear tracks. This is where he feasted: torn bits of seal and walrus skin were scattered all around. Then, right beneath an overhanging ledge, in an indentation sheltered from the wind, we came upon his den. The snow in front of it was packed hard with his footprints, and here and there we could detect yellowish-white hairs from his coat against the whiter snow.

Actually, it was possible to reach the shoreline only at this point, in the region of the station. This we had understood quite clearly as we had circled the island in the helicopter. Yet reaching the shoreline did not at all mean reaching the ocean ice. At the shoreline we encountered an unexpected obstacle: a barrier of ice six meters high sloped toward us, a sort of rampart surrounding the island. Clambering up this pile up of ice boulders, the result of hummocking, we managed to reach the top.

That's where the road ended.

The northern side of the barrier, like a granite embankment, dropped vertically into the ocean. It had been hewn away by drifting ice, planing away all projections, making this side of the rampart a sheer drop.

Noting Dmitri's reaction, I could not help shooting a barb in his direction. "Did you imagine it like this, too?" I chided him.

There was no reply. Dmitri was preoccupied, turning the problem over in his mind.

"Let's not rush to conclusions," he said finally. "We have come this far, and nothing is going to stop us. Nothing!" He paused, and in a while began more quietly. "If you really want to know, I am even quite pleased we have run into such obstacles right at the beginning."

I must have raised an eyebrow at this, because Dmitri became at once more emphatic. "Yes, I am pleased!" he repeated. "Because when we surmount this difficulty, we will be right in the groove; this will mobilize all our will-power and our energy right from the start."

"But how do you plan to set out from here?"

"I cannot believe there is no way out."

"So that means we'll have to wait?"

"We'll look for a way out."

The wall of this embankment dropped not into the open sea, but into the sludge ice we had seen from above. We could see small icebergs the size of a two-storied house scrape the seabed and tumble over, and then the ocean would seem to boil, sending wave after slushy wave into the shore.

"How treacherous you turned out to be, Henrietta," my companion said very softly.

We returned up the steep incline and walked a bit to the east. For some reason known only to himself, Dmitri was excited. He kept looking around, with a bright sparkle in his dark eyes.

"How many times have I imagined myself on this island!" he exclaimed. "And here I am! Everything seems familiar. Right now we are standing on Cape Melville. And over there, beyond the dome of the glacier, is Mt. Chipp. To the left is Cape Bennett, and beyond it Cape Sadko. Do you remember where those names come from?"

"Naturally!"

. . . The discovery of Henrietta Island was connected with the tragic fate of an American polar expedition, headed by Lieutenant George De Long, that one hundred years ago tried to conquer the North Pole. De Long and his thirty-two companions were undoubtedly brave men. This was evident from their plan: to sail through the Bering Strait on board the steam-powered yacht *Jeannette,* and to move as far as possible through the ice; they would then make a dash to the North Pole by dogsled. All this at a time when information about the Arctic, the direction of icefloes, and weather conditions was very scanty indeed. Even large islands and entire archipelagoes had not yet been charted.

These men were heading into the unknown, dooming themselves to almost certain death. Yet the Pole beckoned.

At the beginning, however, De Long was absolutely confident of victory. On July 8, 1879, right before the *Jeannette* set sail, the publisher of the *New York Herald,* James Gordon Bennett, who financed the expedition, presented De Long a copper box on which were engraved the names of the expedition members. The plan was to set this box on the North Pole in a solemn ceremony.

Having passed the shores of the Chukchi Peninsula, the yacht swerved confidently northward.

On September 5, not far from Wrangel Island, the vessel became trapped in powerful pack ice. For an incredible twenty-one months, the *Jeannette* drifted helplessly to the northwest, pulled along by the imprisoning ice. The hull of the yacht creaked and groaned from the pressure of the ice. "We are living on a powder keg, expecting an explosion any moment," De Long wrote in his diary. Their hopes of reaching the area near the Pole had vanished. A year after being trapped, he made the following entry: "During this period, the expedition has drifted only a hundred and fifty miles, and the Pole is still as far away as on the day of our departure. I think we can say goodbye to the North Pole."

On May 16, 1881, the explorers spotted an unknown island. Exhausted by the monotonous struggle against the ice, the captain recorded this event in his diary as "astounding." In honor of the vessel, this tiny bit of land was named Jeannette Island.

A few days later they came upon a second island. This they named Henrietta Island, in honor of their patron's mother. A dogsled team under the command of the ship's chief engineer, a man named Melville, surveyed the open land, compiled a partial description of the island, and set up a landmark, placing inside it a metal tube containing notes.

The island was 4.2 kilometers long, 3.6 kilometers wide. The glacier rising in the center was 312 meters high. Seabirds nested in the cliffs.

On June 12 the vessel was crushed by the ice. Their journey to the Pole ended where ours was to begin. Having saved their warm clothing, rations, and dogs, De Long decided to head back to the mainland. That thousand-kilometer journey made in dogsleds and rowboats stands as one of the most striking exploits in the history of Arctic exploration.

At first Lady Luck was on the side of the explorers: by September they had reached the New Siberian Islands, and were able to replenish their meager stock of meat by hunting. Then in three boats they set out over the open waters of the Laptev Sea for the delta of the Lena River, where they hoped to find a settlement. That night the frail rowboats were tossed about by a sudden storm and lost contact with one another. The boat under the command of Lieutenant Chipp apparently capsized, with all aboard lost without a trace. De Long's party managed to reach the mainland, but except for two sailors he dispatched to the Yakuts for help, they all died there of hunger and cold. Only Melville's party was lucky: having entered one of the tributaries of the Lena, the Americans almost immediately met some local hunters, who helped the sick and weakened sailors reach Yakutsk. Rescue parties were sent out to search for the others, but in vain.

Thus the expedition met its end. For more than half a century no human foot stepped on the islands discovered by the Americans. Not until 1937 did the Soviet icebreaker *Sadko* drop anchor off Henrietta, where it was decided to establish a polar station. On the high shore they built a wooden house, a radio shack, a bathhouse, and a warehouse. Seven men spent the winter there, and while exploring the island, the crew's biologist found, under a seagull's nest, the metal cylinder containing Melville's notes.

Because of the remoteness of the island—at times dense ice prevented vessels reaching the island even in summer—and since there was nowhere for aircraft to land, it was decided eventually to "mothball" the station on Henrietta. So once again the only masters here were polar bears.

Since De Long's time, the number of human beings to visit these majestic cliffs could be counted on one's hands.

By the time Dmitri and I returned to the station, the others had everything shipshape. The stoves were burning nicely, and Melnikov had made radio contact with the base at Kotelny. He had informed Labutin that the start of the expedition was being postponed for a day.

Dusk had set in. On a shelf, among books and magazines gone yellow with time, I found a package of candles. It was difficult to say how old they were, but they still burned well enough. The coals crackled in the stoves, and the light of the flames, peeking through the grates, danced on the ceiling. It was warm and very near cozy.

By nightfall, it had become much colder. When I went outdoors for a minute, I could hardly catch my breath for the wind. Out on the ocean the ice rumbled in a dull, threatening tone, while to the west the sky was still tinted blood-red going to dark purple. It was awe-inspiring. In that picture you could find nothing down-to-earth, nothing related to the warm fragrance of grass and the chirping of birds. Only in the knowledge that nearby was a house, full of warmth and good friends, could you look upon the sight without fear. Even so, I hurried back to the building.

Supper was short. Unlike our usual mealtime chit-chat, the conversation at table seemed rather distracted. Each man, in his own mind already on the move, was wondering how it would go, was weighing everything he had seen that day.

At five the next morning, Oleg and I began getting breakfast. By six everyone was up and about. After oatmeal and meat, washed down with black coffee, everyone seemed finally awake, and in a noticeably merrier mood.

"We start out in an hour," Dmitri announced for the second time. "It seems to me that not all of you will be ready."

Khmelevsky and Ledenev, the objects of Shparo's indirection, preferred to say nothing. Vladimir was fiddling around with the tool kit, while Yuri seemed to be moving in slow motion so as not to forget anything.

"Hey, men," he raised his head from his rucksack. "What's your attitude to garlic? Do we take some along or not?"

The team seemed agreed it was a great idea. "Gotta have garlic," someone said. Only Rakhmanov said nothing—he could not abide the stuff.

"But why do you ask?" Dmitri asked warily. "You know it's included in our rations."

"Sure, I know that," Yuri agreed quite readily. "But I forgot it at Kotelny."

Everyone burst out laughing, including Dmitri, who quickly enough remembered to frown. "I hope that's the only thing you've forgotten," he said.

"I'd like to believe in that too," Yuri agreed.

No longer did Dmitri hurry anyone. As usual, when he wanted to get his message across to others, he resorted to his tested method of setting a personal example. He quickly packed his rucksack and put on his warm clothing. Some five meters from the house, he put on his skis and, without looking back, headed toward the ocean. The rest of us followed right behind.

During the night, the ice conditions had grown worse. The river of crushed ice was twice as wide, and to the west of the island patches of open water had appeared. Everything here changed so swiftly that, in an hour's time, instead of these patches of open water there might well be found ridges and hummocks of ice.

Skiing down to the shoreline, we discarded our rucksacks and clambered up the rampart. This was a time for action, for decisiveness, but for the moment everyone seemed rooted to the spot. Seemingly bewitched, we stood there at the edge of the precipice, while below, the ocean, like a giant beast, writhed, stirred, and boiled.

Floating past us some fifty meters offshore was a huge chunk of pack ice, actually a small iceberg, covered with hummocks hollowed out by the sun. All of a sudden it came to a standstill, probably having scraped the seabed. Almost immediately, an ice jam formed. Chunks of ice started piling up against the iceberg, instantly freezing the sludge into a bridge of ice. The thought that sprang into all our minds was not to miss this moment: scurry across to the iceberg and then make a further dash while the sludge still held. The whole team came to life; some had already taken off their skis, while others scurried back to pick up their rucksacks. All of a sudden, though, an ear-splitting noise forced everyone's gaze toward the ocean. The iceberg, which only a minute ago seemed to us the only dependable and stable island in the whole area, had under the impact of some unknown force heaved slowly upward and turned over. From textbooks we knew that the submerged part of an iceberg is some ten times greater than the part above the surface—and now we could see this with our own eyes. The island of ice tumbled over slowly—I would even say, majestically. Torrents of water streamed down walls of blue ice. Huge chunks breaking off the berg splashed thunderously into the water only to be swirled downward into icy vortices. And then suddenly everything around the iceberg went once again into motion. I am probably not the only one there that day who shuddered at the thought of what would have happened had we at that moment been on the ice.

"Ice recon patrol!" Dmitri ordered, taking charge of the situation. "Vasili and Anatoli must find a way down to the sea, and see if we can cross the sludge. Their back-up man is Vadim. The rest of us will go toward that patch of open water, to see if we can cross by boat. And step on it, men, time is running short."

"The boss of the Arctic has been waiting for you on the other side for quite some time," remarked Oleg, point-ing to a spot across the river of sludge. There a polar bear was stalking about, probably on the trail of some seal. He seemed absolutely indifferent to our plight.

For a time, the three of us—Oleg, Alexander, and myself—remained alone. I recall that the most vivid sen-sation during those moments was a great desire to hide somewhere from the cold and the wind. Over my face I pulled a woolen ski mask, like a terrorist's hood, with narrow eye slits. I found a secluded little trench between

71

hummocks, and tumbled into it like a bear into his den. Here at least the wind was not so exasperating. If one could believe the thermometer, the temperature was minus thirty. However, in the Arctic it is more correct to use a scale that takes wind velocity into account, what is called the wind-chill factor. By this scale, the temperature was the equivalent of minus sixty.

Nearby, Sasha was busy reloading his cameras. Now and again, dangerous white spots would appear on his face. "Rub your cheeks!" we would shout. Obediently, he would rub his cheeks with his mittens. A couple of minutes later, the spots would reappear, and again we would shout. Sasha became a bit nervous because he could not do two things at once. In the end, he decided to sacrifice his cheeks, which were severely frostbitten as a result. The traces were noticeable on his face for several months afterwards.

Suddenly the whirring and whistling of a chopper could be heard overhead: the MI-8 had arrived. It made two passes the length of the island and then gently floated down to the same spot it had landed yesterday. Heading down toward us were the cameramen and Victor Krivosheya. The latter asked no questions—everything was clear to him. He puffed on his cigaret and stared sullenly at the ice. Apparently he thought that all this could only end badly.

"Did you see anything significant from above?" I asked.

"The same damn thing," Krivosheya shrugged his shoulders. "Listen, perhaps we lift them over this sludge in the chopper? Who's to know?"

I spread out my hand reproachfully. "Victor, you know we made an agreement."

"All right, all right, I take it back. I just feel sorry for those boys."

We had anticipated such suggestions and were ready

for them. For the pilots it seemed entirely logical to use the helicopter to lift the group to firm ice. They reasoned, something like the following: "What are a few hundred meters when there are a whole fifteen hundred kilometers ahead of you? So the skiers don't start from the island itself, so what? So they start from good pack ice as near the land as possible—what's the difference? This way the risk will be minimal."

But as reasonable as this might sound, we could not agree. Such an arrangement would compromise the whole expedition. First of all, it ran counter to the whole idea of the journey: *from Soviet shores to the Pole.* From the shore! Second, it would significantly alter the physiological experiment we were undertaking, one of the main conditions of which was that the group was to be totally autonomous. And above all else, the "helicopter variant" would be unwise because in the future it might give rise to rumors that the expedition was constantly accompanied by a helicopter that lifted the skiers across open water and hummocks. Rumors are a dangerous thing. If there is even the slightest basis for them, it becomes impossible to defend oneself.

We are not the only expedition to have run into a problem like this. Wally Herbert, the British explorer whose journey by dogsled in 1968–69 was the first trans-Atlantic passage, encountered similar obstacles. He and three of his companions were to finish their trek on board the H.M.S. *Endurance,* which was locked into the ice not far from Spitsbergen and considered part of British territory. They were only forty miles from the vessel when ice conditions became suddenly worse. The four men and their dogs floundered among the piles of hummocked ice for days, making practically no headway at all. By radio, the captain of the ship insisted on evacuation of the group by helicopter. Herbert categorically refused, claiming that this would irreparably compromise the last leg of the expedition. Again the captain insisted on their evacuation: "The vessel cannot wait amid ice capable of crushing it." This, one had to agree, was a strong argument, and Herbert gave in. A helicopter was sent for them, but Herbert will no doubt regret that painful necessity all his life.

Both groups returned from ice reconnaissance patrol. Melnikov reported, with disappointment in his voice, that it would be impossible to cross the sludge, while Ledenev's information was hardly more consoling. The open water they had examined was bounded on one side by the sheer cliffs of Henrietta and on the other by a very high and steep barrier of ice. The descent to the water would pose a real problem, even for experienced mountain climbers. And as if that were not bad enough, right in front of the reconnaissance team the water began to freeze, to thicken into a kind of gruel, something half water and half ice that would be both tortuous and dangerous to cross.

More than an hour had passed since the group had made its descent to the shoreline. The situation now seemed hopeless. I myself was thinking that the start would probably have to be postponed. Why take chances the first day out?

Everyone was silent, and kept looking around. No one offered any ideas or advice, for the simple reason that no one could think of anything. As for Dmitri, he looked a bit dismayed. It seemed to me he was trying to avoid our eyes, as at this point everyone was looking to him for leadership and he felt as lost as we did.

Then, simple as that, a large piece of ice resembling a raft floated up to the foot of the rampart right where we were standing, and with squeaks and groans came to a stop. All motion on our river had again come to a standstill. Another ice jam had formed "downstream."

"All right, men, we start here," Dmitri uttered these words not too loudly.

TREACHEROUS HENRIETTA

Out of his breast pocket Ledenev produced a strong kapron cord. Vasili tied it around his waist for safety, and slowly began lowering himself. In a minute, he was already boldly strutting about the "raft," and was quickly followed by Rakhmanov. Meanwhile, Oleg and I began hauling the rucksacks to the top of the rampart. Never in my life, it seemed, had I performed such hard work. To hoist a fifty-kilo rucksack up this steep, slippery incline was a tough job even for two men. That was when I finally realized the full extent of the burden my friends had taken on.

However, there was not much time right then to reflect on my realization. Already six men had made it safely to the ice raft, and only Khmelevsky remained on the rampart. We helped him lower rucksacks, skis, ski poles, carbine to the floating piece of ice, and then lowered Yuri himself. The entire operation lasted a matter of minutes.

At this point the expedition was officially under way.

And only when all seven were below us did I realize we had not said our goodbyes. It was very disappointing. We had not even shaken hands. The men on the ice raft suddenly realized this too, and we shouted encouraging words to one another in parting. Then someone fired several flares into the sky, and that was all. . . . They were off.

Photographer Sasha Abazha, who by that time had forgotten about his hopelessly frostbitten face, was clicking away with all three of his cameras. Later on, he admitted to me that never before in all his twenty years of work had he witnessed anything like this. He was simply astounded by the events unfolding before him and yearned to capture it all on film.

Actually, I regretted there were no TV cameras on the island that day. How many people around the world might have watched, with bated breath, the dramatic beginning of the first Pole-bound ski journey in history: truly this was a spectacle deserving of worldwide coverage.

Having left their skies behind on the ice raft, the men started out in Indian file across the shaky and undulating mash toward the large chunk of pack ice that had stopped in its tracks some hundred meters to the northwest. They proceeded with caution, carefully testing each step. In the meantime, the three of us watching from the shore had become chilled through and through; yet how could we return to the house at a moment like this?

When they were but a few meters from the pack ice, the men encountered water—a narrow channel, half filled with sludge, made further progress impossible. They had first to engineer a crossing. Off came their rucksacks. Using chunks of ice they clogged the passage and laid their skis across it; then, with the kapron cord, they pulled the rucksacks over this bridge and after that crossed it themselves. Seeing them safely on the icefloe, we on the shore heaved a collective sigh of relief. Then they split into two groups: five of them scattered over the island of ice in search of a way to continue their journey, while Melnikov and Rakhmanov, now without their packs, returned to the ice raft for their skis.

"Anatoli! How is it?" I shouted when they were below us.

"Bearable," Melnikov replied, with deliberate understatement and a modulated cheerfulness.

Obviously excited, he was humming something to himself. Rakhmanov's excitement took a different form: quietly intense, he did not even look up at us.

"So long, guys!" one of us shouted as they were about to leave. And then the rest of us joined in.

"Till we meet at the Pole!"

"We're with you all the way!"

In reply, Anatoli waved weakly, while Vladimir did not even raise his head. I think in his concentration he did not even hear us.

"Good luck to you! May the ice be smooth and the sun warm!"

TREACHEROUS HENRIETTA

The vicious cold whipped the tears out of our eyes. We kept watching as the dark figures drew further and further from the land. They had entered into a life-and-death struggle with the Arctic and would have to fight for every meter on their way to the Pole. Step by step. The fight had begun at nine in the morning, local time. And now it was two in the afternoon. They had one and a half million meters left to go.

Once, while in Rome, I visited the Coliseum. This gigantic structure served the Imperial Romans as a gladiatorial arena in which slaves, as a public entertainment, fought to the death either against each other or against wild beasts. The spectators, for safety's sake, sat well above the carnage—all that spilling of blood took place as if at the bottom of a well. And now, watching from above how my comrades gave battle to the Arctic ice, I remembered the Coliseum. There was no danger to us, up here in the stands, while below, just a few score meters away, our friends were risking their lives. And there was nothing we could do to make it any easier for them. Just sit back and watch. Torture yourself, if you will, with the thought that you are not with them, that it is not you challenging the Arctic, that it is not under your skis that the crushed ice is even now quivering.

I looked up out of my reverie to find Krivosheya was looking at me inquiringly. He had just come down to fetch us.

"Time to fly out, eh, Victor?" I asked.

"Just about. The chopper can't stand in such cold for more than a couple of hours. The props will freeze up."

Carefully, with the toe of his boot, he stubbed out his unfinished cigaret, and smiled guiltily: "The commander's already getting fidgety. He's afraid we might have to spend the winter here."

"Well, spending the winter on Henrietta does not enter our plan. Right, Oleg?"

I turned toward Obukhov, who seemed deep in a reverie of his own.

"Yes." He squeezed the word out of himself distractedly and continued gazing northward. "We'll have plenty of work on our hands now, that's for sure."

Sasha, the poor devil, by now almost frozen stiff, had gone up to the house before us. Not much of a talker to begin with, he had hardly uttered a word the entire day. However shellshocked he may have appeared, though, he kept as busy as ever with his cameras. For their part, the TV cameramen were on the verge of tears: their cameras categorically refused to work in such cold.

Taking our time and casting a backward glance every once in a while, we descended the rampart, walked past the bear's den, and began the climb up to the polar station. As we looked the tiny figures of our comrades seemed particularly defenseless against the chaos of hummocks, crevices, and icebergs that surrounded them.

Only later, much later, did we learn of the adventures that befell them that day.

On the iceberg they had reached they were again brought to a standstill: on its north side, chunks of ice mixed with snowy sludge floated by in a stream as swift and broad as the one they had just crossed. From the experience of that day they knew to wait for the next ice jam. In such bitter cold even the slightest halt rendered the sludge passable, freezing it almost instantly. The team managed in this way to cross to the next berg, and this encouraged them. They knew that before nightfall they had to make it to a solid ice field. They were in a hurry.

They were headed for a large icefloe some fifty meters to the northwest; it stood out like an aircraft carrier amid tugboats. The first man in line was Vasili. Hopping and skipping from one piece of ice to another was right up his alley. "As a boy, every spring I ice-rafted along our river," he had told us. "Our river, like our town, has the name

Lepsy. It's no wider than the Moskva River, but it's much faster."

Only a few meters from the icefloe, Vasili was standing on a tiny piece of pack ice. In his right hand were his skis, in his left the poles, on his back his rucksack. And in his heart a sense of self-congratulation. What a dashing fellow! A newcomer to the expedition, yet always up in front—a real trailblazer. Just watch! He'd show everyone how to cope with the ice. Dmitri is too slow. He wastes too much time weighing things in his mind. You must act more boldly and more resolutely. Like this. Probe the ice in front with skis and poles. It seems to hold. What's the use of taking it slowly? Here goes.

No sooner had his feet touched the ice than Vasili realized he was going under. The crust proved no stronger than a waffle. Almost before he knew it, he was in water right up to his rucksack. Until one of these sacks becomes soaked, it can keep a person afloat, just like a lifejacket. But at the same time, with fifty kilos on your back there is no getting out of the water. To free himself, Vasili let go of his skis. At once he was benumbed—not from the freezing-cold water, but at the sight of what happened next. Plop! Straight to the bottom went his skis. Quickly he slipped off his rucksack, only to have the horrible thought pass through his mind: "It seems the rucksack went down too." He did not give even a thought to the possibility that the next instant he might suffer a similar fate. Now I've done it, was all he could think; now they'll send me back to the island for sure.

Meanwhile he was floundering in water up to his neck, trying to waddle his way to solid ice, smashing the half-frozen sludge into small bits and leaving behind him a wake of open water. He had been in the drink now for a couple of minutes, his companions far behind suspecting nothing.

In the tent that evening they would reproach him. "Why didn't you yell out, Vasili?" they said.

"Because I was not scared," replied our hero. "There was no time for that."

"Well, you're brave enough, that's for sure," Melnikov noted severely, "but your little dip almost wrecked the whole expedition. You mustn't think only of yourself."

But it was Rakhmanov who lashed out with the most stinging words: "Mountain climbers have a golden rule: if you fall, you yell out. Whether you're scared or not, you yell out anyway. But not you, oh no. What do you do. . .?"

"I've never *been* a mountain climber," Vasili snapped back. "And I don't *know* the rules of mountain climbing. All my life I've traveled alone, and have had to rely only on myself." But his answer lacked conviction—he was only trying to save face. It was clear to us all that Vasili knew he was wrong.

. . . Swimming up to the icefloe, he grabbed the edge and tried to pull himself up. No luck: the edge broke off, and he almost went under completely. One more try. This time he no longer attempted to pull himself onto the ice; instead he simply held on so as not to drown. He looked to the right: sure enough, Shparo and Ledenev were coming on the run. "Hold on," they cried. They had thrown off their rucksacks and were circumventing the thin ice as quickly as they could. When they made it to the ice floe they flopped on their bellies at the water's edge, threw off their mittens, and with extended arms grabbed Vasili by the wrists. In an instant they had yanked him out of the water; in another they had retrieved his rucksack and ski poles.

But even as water streamed down Vasili's clothing another mishap occurred: now it was Khmelevsky who almost drowned himself. Yuri himself explained it: "All day I felt as though I were walking in my sleep, as if I were being carried on the crest of a wave. But where to? And why? I didn't for the life of me know. Once we had left Henrietta behind and I felt the quivering ice underfoot, I thought to myself: well, old man, that's it, there's no turning back. You've stuck your foot into this thing, and how it's going to end no one knows. I was in that state all the time, hardly realizing what was happening all around us.

"I was walking behind Dmitri when he saw Vasili floundering about in the water. I didn't see him swimming or even how he was rescued. I had a vague sense of Dmitri running wildly about, but I didn't know why. Bewildered, and simply by inertia, I took several more steps. Then, all of a sudden, the piece of ice under me started sinking. In an instant, I was in water up to my chest. I grabbed hold of a chunk of ice and quite calmly began thinking, not about myself, but as if I were observing someone else: 'Well, that is how death comes.' These sad thoughts were quickly interrupted by Melnikov and Rakhmanov. Ordering me to slide the rucksack off my back, they lost no time pulling me out of the water.

"I just stood there on the ice, not feeling the cold at all, though I was soaking wet. Nearby, Vasili was pouring the water out of his boots. The others were probing the sludge with ski poles, hoping that Vasili's skis had not gone down, and that they would find them. Dmitri simply shrugged his shoulders and shook his head. 'Well, guys,' he said, 'if we ever make it to the Pole. . . .' "

Back on Henrietta we had reached the helicopter. The mechanic was already revving the engine, and soon we were headed out to sea in the direction of the ski team. One of the cameramen, secured in a harness, was leaning out the open hatch. The idea was to have the chopper hover twenty meters or so above the skiers, and then gradually zoom upward; the men on the ice would grow smaller and smaller until they dissolved altogether against a background of endless white.

Vasili, hearing and then seeing the helicopter descending, lost heart completely. He thought that for himself the expedition was over. Dmitri would order him to say goodbye to his comrades, and he would be flown back to the mainland. His clothing had by now turned into an icy suit of armor, and water sloshed in his boots. But he did not feel the cold. As if bewitched, he alternated his gaze between the helicopter hovering directly above him, and Dmitri, who was giving some kind of hand signal to the pilot.

All of a sudden, the roaring and whistling intensified; the downdraft from the rotor became so powerful it seemed the icefloe would capsize any moment. The chopper rapidly gained altitude, and in a few seconds seemed little more than a barely audible dragonfly. The men on the ice waved their hands as the cameraman had instructed them, while Vasili tried to make himself inconspicuous. He hardly dared believe that the trouble had quite literally blown over, and that he would be allowed to continue.

That was the view from below. From the helicopter we could see the group moving slowly about as we first approached them. Their thick parkas, looking like spacesuits, gave them the appearance of cosmonauts, while the landscape looked even less terrestrial. Below us, Dmitri was shouting something we could not hear, and made signs with his hands: I could make out something about their having lost a ski. Only several days later did we learn by radio that a pair of skis had gone to the bottom. Then the cameraman began shooting and yelled to the pilot to lift the chopper straight up. Gradually the men on the ice became barely visible specks, finally fading into the endless Arctic white.

As we headed for the mainland, we remained silent for a long time. Finally, I opened my diary and began scribbling the text of the official dispatch to expedition headquarters.

Moscow, *Komsomolskaya Pravda*, to: Ganichev, Mokrousov. On March 16, 1979, at 0200 hours Moscow time, the ski team of the expedition, consisting of Dmitri Shparo, Yuri Khmelevsky, Anatoli Melnikov, Vladimir Ledenev, Vladimir Rakhmanov, Vadim Davydov, and Vasili Shishkarev, started from Henrietta Island. According to plan, the team is heading for the geographic North Pole. Air temperature in starting region: minus thirty. Ice reconnaissance of the initial part of the route performed by MI-8 helicopter. Base camp radio station on Kotelny Island is in contact with the ski team and with Moscow. All members of the expedition send their greetings, and are determined to fulfill their mission. Congratulations to all.

The expedition found themselves unable to pitch camp on the icefloe they had reached—it was much too insecure. Moreover, it was moving rapidly westward. Yuri and Vasili, probably to redeem themselves, readily agreed to continue marching, without taking time to change into dry clothing.

Marching about an hour, they found themselves on another large icefloe, this one drifting to the northwest. On three sides, it was surrounded by vast expanses of open water. Dusk was falling.

"This is it," declared Dmitri, coming to a halt. "We spend the night here."

Vadim looked concerned. "I wonder," he drawled, "where we'll end up in the morning."

"Yeah," Anatoli put in, "the speed this thing's going, any overnight shift of direction could put us farther from the Pole than we are right now."

"Precisely," said Vadim. "At the very least, a drift like this could have us marking time forever."

"Let's just sleep on it, fellas," Yuri philosophized. He

was ripping away at his parka, which had become frozen to his sweater. "Since none of us drowned, we can consider it to have been a simply wonderful day."

As if hiding behind the distant hummocks, the unblinking sun seemed to be sizing them up. Its Cyclops eye of molten red looked especially ominous that moment.

"We Seem to Be Freezing into the Ice"

The polar journeys Shparo has organized over the years
have one thing in common. Their first days have always
been the most difficult and hazardous. No sooner would
the team don their skis and set out than there ensued one
misadventure after another. It seemed almost as if the
North wanted to check the credentials of anyone who
dared enter.

In 1971, we had barely started our trek across Severnaya Zemlya when a terrific gale came up, strong
enough to knock a man off his feet. For two days it raged,
ripping our tent to shreds and threatening to break our
spirit. We were able to cover a mere seven kilometers.
Only when we began to forget our sufferings, and to act
as if we had no intention of turning back, did the wind
finally relent.

The next year, our expedition ventured out onto drifting ice north of Chukchi, in Long Strait. Here was the ideal "model" of the Arctic basin, a perfect proving ground. Try to picture a stretch of the Arctic Ocean some two hundred kilometers wide and clogged with ice even in summer. It offered us hummocks, patches of open water, crevices hidden by snow, a fast-moving drift—in short, the entire gamut of hazards we would meet on our way to the Pole.

And here, as before, we were not spared our cruel initiation. Witness these excerpts from my diary, recorded in the spring of 1972:

"*April 8.* Second day of the journey. The hummocks seem endless. Zigzagging all the time . . . circumventing the hummocks, clambering up them like mountain climbers, falling into crevices. We pitch camp before a new ridge of icy hummocks. We shudder at the thought of what awaits us tomorrow.

"*April 9.* Once again hummocks all the way. The weather has taken a turn for the worse: wind, snow, white mist. The barometer is falling; soon we can expect a real snowstorm. Really tough moving across stretches of newly broken ice—negotiating these bare slabs can be compared to walking a tightrope.

"*April 10.* Debris of smashed ice all around us, an impassable, hopeless bedlam. We are barely crawling. . . . 'It seems that with every step we take, we are tightening the noose around our neck,' jokes Khmelevsky, not without gloom in his voice. Amid the general chaos of ice, it is with great difficulty that we find even a tiny piece of solid ice to stand on.'

Several more days were recorded in the diary in the same spirit. A week after we had started out, I came down with pneumonia, aggravated, I am sure, by the hopelessly heavy work of crossing that icy nightmare. A helicopter had to be summoned by radio to evacuate, besides myself, Fyodor Sklokin, who was suffering terribly from fits of snowblindness. The journey to Wrangel Island was completed by only five men.

"That damned strait!" I wrote in the hospital. "It broke me down. To fall ill just when the most difficult part of the journey was completed. . . . It looked like defeat. I can explain my departure to my friends, to the pilots, to the doctors—they will understand me, and consider it reasonable, but it is impossible to explain it to myself. Long Strait proved to be stronger than I was. By helicopter it took us half an hour to return to base camp, yet on skis it took seven days to cover the same distance. . . . Damn! Should I respect that strait? Hate it? Forget it?"

To forget it, as you can tell, was impossible.

And four years later, in the spring of 1976, the expedition encountered an almost identical situation. A six-man team—Shparo, Khmelevsky, Ledenev, Davydov, Rakhmanov, and Tenyakshev—started from the northern shore of Wrangel Island and set out across the ocean for NP-23. This was a bold step. No one had ever attempted to ski from solid land to this polar station adrift in an ocean of ice. No sooner had the party set out than they ran into a horrible mess, the Wrangel polynya, a huge field of plowed-up ice stretching scores of kilometers in every direction. The hummocks here sometimes towered as high as ten meters.

The group seemed hopelessly stuck just beyond the ice-shelf abutting the island. In five days, they had covered little more than twenty kilometers. They were giving it all they had, working twelve hours a day, but still made little headway. With almost three hundred kilometers still to go, they had food and fuel for only twenty-four days. The plan of the expedition did not include airdrops.

Finally, one very long week later, the Arctic took mercy on the group. But first it had tested them with dangerous crossings over open water, with sudden cracks in the ice, with attacks by polar bears. Through all of this, not one of the six had faltered even for a moment. No one was faint-hearted, no one thought of giving up. And when finally the ice became smoother, they made up for lost time and in a total of twenty-two days completed their trek to NP-23. I shall never forget the spectacle of their arrival: the six emerged out of a white snowstorm as if being developed on photographic paper, and then headed casually over to the small buildings of the station.

And now, the Arctic had remained true to itself. The passage to the Pole was beginning with a series of tests equally cruel.

The team was now half a kilometer from Henrietta, on a small icefloe scudding swiftly northwestward. Fatigued by the cold, and by their heavy and dangerous work, the men got down to pitching camp, with none of the usual conversation. At that moment they wanted only to get warm, to feel solid ice beneath their feet, and to have a good sleep.

In the tent, various members of the team offered dry clothing to Vasili and Yuri, but the two "bathers" seemed a bit shamefaced, and the attention made them uncomfortable. Their teeth chattered as they hung up, wherever they could, their wet socks and underwear, and the parkas crusted over with ice.

By now Anatoli had the transmitter going, and very soon the first radio contact was made between ski team and base camp.

"Situation complicated. Everything okay. Have covered five hundred meters," Melnikov reported.

"How much?" Labutin could not believe his ears. It seemed so little.

"Five hundred. Five-zero-zero," Melnikov confirmed. "Goodbye for now."

The microphone was then taken over by Vadim Davydov, who was on assignment for the medical periodical

Meditsinskaya Gazetta. In an even tone he began dictating his coverage of the first day. Though he reported the "dips" taken by two of the party, he omitted any mention of their names so as not to alarm their relatives.

Meanwhile, Ledenev went about fulfilling his obligations as the man on KP that evening.

"Hey, guys, who's got the matches?" he inquired.

A moment of confusion ensued. For some reason, everyone thought Khmelevsky should have matches.

"Well," shrugged Yuri, "if you consider me responsible for lighting the fire, I do not object."

"Then out with the matches, Prometheus," exclaimed Ledenev, impatiently drumming his fingers on the bright orange primus stove.

"Matches?" said Yuri. "I have no matches. I only now learned the fire's my responsibility."

At this, every jaw in camp dropped in amazement.

"Probably the matches were left behind at Henrietta," Yuri offered. "I'll run over in a jiffy."

This proposal set off a peal of laughter. Immediately jaws were put in gear again. "Run over to Henrietta!" Everyone was smiling and chuckling. Fortunately the provident Ledenev, back in Moscow, had thought to bring along an extra box of matches just in case.

"Well, guys," said Khmelevsky through chattering teeth, "if it weren't for that box of matches, we'd have to turn back."

"Why?" demanded Vasili, looking up reproachfully. "There are more ways than one to light a fire."

"Like rubbing two pieces of ice together," mocked Anatoli. But it was not so easy to knock Vasili off balance.

"What are the batteries for?" he asked. "A small short circuit and you've got a spark, then a flame. So step right up and get warm."

Then Yuri climbed out of the tent, clambered up an

old hummock, and surveyed the scene around him. The icefloe they were on continued to drift quite rapidly to the northwest. Vast expanses of open water could be seen to the north. We didn't see that from the helicopter yesterday, Yuri reflected. Over in the direction the current was carrying them stretched a veritable sea, its opposite shore shrouded in thick fog. Yuri wondered if fate might not hold an unexpected twist in store for them. If the drift indeed did happen to reverse itself, they might soon find themselves off the shores of Siberia instead of on their way to the North Pole. This unpleasant thought was interrupted by a voice coming from the tent. Ledenev was calling him to supper.

Once, while sitting around the table on some festive occasion a long while back, we all began characterizing one another in culinary terms:

"You remind me of a lemon—talking to you I become bitter."

"You're like champagne—you bubble and boil, but not for long."

In the course of this banter, Khmelevsky was called "sugar with salt." Yuri was quite pleased with the analogy, believing it fitted him to a tee.

Personally, it did not strike me at the time as terribly apt. Only later, when reflecting on the character of my friend, did I understand why Yuri had so readily embraced the epithet.

He is absolutely unpredictable. Today he is "sugar," tomorrow "salt." It is practically impossible to draw a verbal portrait of him. His character, his thoughts, are exceedingly elusive.

What can be said about him with certainty is the following. In the expedition, Khmelevsky performs three important functions: he is scientific leader, navigator, and dietitian. Each of these roles is tremendously important.

Right from the beginning, we were called upon to conduct a large number of scientific investigations. As time went on, the number of agencies and institutes co-operating with the expedition grew apace. The responsibility for coordinating our comprehensive scientific program and for preparing the expedition's scientific report rests on the shoulders of Khmelevsky.

The post of navigator obliges Yuri to know the most intricate details of navigation in the upper latitudes, to skillfully use the sextant, the theodolite, the compass. To determine one's position and chart a course in the Arctic—where there are no landmarks, where the ice is in constant motion, where the meridians converge into a tight bundle—is a task of unusual complexity. One of the oldest Soviet navigators, Nikolai Zhukov, a man who in 1937 participated in landing Ivan Papanin's group at the Pole, once paid Yuri a great compliment: "Your navigator knows his business," he said. "He handles the theodolite like a violin."

Needless to say, food is an important component of any life-supporting system for people working in the Arctic. All our rations must weigh as little as possible while containing maximum caloric content and a good balance of fats, proteins, and carbohydrates. After many years of experimenting, Khmelevsky was able to develop a diet we can confidently recommend to all who travel and work in the upper latitudes.

If Dmitri is the heart of the expedition, Yuri is its soul. He is close to everyone, and everyone relies on him. Our scientific leader tries to keep in the shadows, and never tries to foist his ideas on anyone, but Shparo will never make an important decision without him. Like an ancient sage, Yuri avoids categorical formulations; on every question he has a profound desire to get to the crux of the matter. He has been known to call himself an analyst, though always with a trace of irony.

In 1966 Khmelevsky defended his dissertation on the topic "Equations in Words." The scientific council of the Mechanico-Mathematics Department at Moscow University acknowledged it an outstanding contribution to mathematics. Though his work has been translated into many languages, he has never fully developed his mathematical talent. Science requires an almost single-minded dedication, while Yuri has divided the past ten years of his life among mathematics, the expedition, and his family. He in fact loves to emphasize his almost fanatic loyalty to household chores and the raising of his children. The father of two girls and a boy, he receives tremendous satisfaction from sitting round the clock at the bedside of a slightly ill child, running around doing the family shopping, or cultivating the vegetable garden at his country home. (Usually, it should be remarked, there is no real need for his sitting up; in the shops he will almost certainly buy items that are not really needed; and nothing, not even weeds, will grow in his garden.)

Perhaps the key to Khmelevsky's character is the fact that he seems to derive pleasure from overcoming hardship and discomfort. He is one of those of whom it used to be said they enjoy bearing the cross.

"Skiing across the ice, I relax both mentally and physically." That's what he says, but it is not to be believed. Those who know him well have learned that in Yuri's mouth certain utterances must be understood as their exact opposite. Some of his habits it is impossible to fathom at all. He may go to the theater wearing a tattered old cap, in work clothes, even with a rucksack on his back. If not intercepted, he may set out for a reception in sweatsuit and running shoes.

"Yuri," I keep on asking him, "why do you insist on looking like a scarecrow?"

"I don't understand you, Vladimir," he replies with genuine amazement. "My sweatsuit is practically new, and my cap—well, my wife is fond of it."

Dmitri has long ago given him up as a lost cause.

"My willpower is based on the concept of patience," Yuri once explained to me. (I had just expressed my great surprise at the way he handled a theodolite; his fingers seemed to cling too tightly to the cold metal.)

"Aren't you being a bit passive?" I scoffed. "Jesus suffered, and willed that we should suffer too."

"Don't confound things," Yuri reproached me. "You and I are talking about very concrete things—one's attitude toward hardships. And in a very specific case—hardships typical of polar expeditions."

"For instance, working with a theodolite?"

"Exactly. Sometimes I really do have to show patience and suffer with a theodolite—for instance, when my hands can no longer feel the instrument. When my fingers are frostbitten. I told myself long ago: you must work exactly as long as necessary. Sometimes there is no other way out."

"Listen, Yuri, you must confess that the pain and the cold bother you. You're no superman!"

"I'm not sure what you mean, 'superman.' I have simply taught myself to put the damper on certain negative emotions. Pain, for example. In essence, this is a pragmatic concept—it prevents excess expenditure of energy."

"All right, let me ask you this: what depresses you most of all on skiing expeditions? The heavy rucksack? The cold? The white mist?"

"None of those. No, what weighs most heavily on my mind are things that remain undone back home, and thoughts about my loved ones. And what's worst of all is trying to sleep at night. My nose gets blocked up, and I have difficulty breathing. A runny nose is not all that harmless. Because of a head cold, Napoleon lost the battle of Waterloo."

"So what does the trek to the Pole mean for you

93

personally? Setting a record? Satisfying your vanity? An unusual adventure?"

"For me it is first of all the fulfillment of our program. But it is also something that fits in with my character. I view this trek to the Pole as the very quintessence of moral, cultural, spiritual power and expressivenss."

"And how do you picture the finish?"

"First, it will be a sunny day; otherwise we wouldn't be able to fix our position and wouldn't know whether we were at the Pole or not. We'll throw off our rucksacks, and the radiomen will set up their equipment to report our victory. And I'll organize a little soccer game right at the North Pole."

Yuri is probably the best soccer player among us. If it were not for his poor eyesight he would be a real asset to even the best teams. However, it was precisely soccer that recently played him a nasty trick. Some six months before the start from Henrietta, Yuri was playing in a game for the institute where he works. In the heat of the game, he did not notice a large hole in the field and sprained his knee very badly. The pain was so great that for a time he lost consciousness. In the hospital, they put a plaster cast on his leg and told him to forget about all action connected with heavy loads. But here he was preparing for the trek to the Pole. A month before the start, Khmelevsky asked me to put him in touch with a famous orthopedist.

"So you want to ski to the North Pole?" the doctor said.

"Yes, I do," said Yuri.

"I will not give my permission for this."

"That's a pity." Yuri was sincerely disappointed. "But if my health is okay, then you can't really stop me."

The orthopedist examined the knee again very carefully, knocking on it and doing all those other things doctors do.

"Get up, you can go."

"Go where?" Yuri did not understand. "Home?"

"To the Pole. Your health is in perfect order."

That very evening Yuri turned up at our training session at the gym and—wouldn't you know?—sprained the same knee. This time the injury was not as bad, but even so his participation in the expedition hung by a thread. He arrived on Kotelny Island tormented by doubts—"If I go with the team, will I let my comrades down?" Only after long consultations with Davydov did he decide to take a crack at the Pole. Yuri himself claims that the final word was that of his wife, Rita. Before his departure from Moscow, she had told him, "You must go. Go, and that's all there is to it. Even with that bum leg of yours. Go!"

And now here he was lying in a sleeping bag, soaked and chilled to the bone, trying to realize what had happened. I fell through the ice, Yuri thought to himself. It was an absurd, even inscrutable occurrence. Inevitable. Irremediable. Nothing I could do to change it. And what if this breaks me? What if I lose my willpower, my drive to keep going, keep struggling? I won't want to get up and leave the tent. What if that's programmed as my destiny? Absurd, silly, idiotic."

That evening Yuri had given no indication he was not himself. He in fact made a show of bravery and had tried to give Ledenev a hand with the chores. But now that everyone was quietly dozing off, it was possible to unbridle his doubts.

The warmer he became, the fewer the doubts. It is necessary to look at things soberly, he thought to himself. What after all really happened? Two men went for a swim. Never before has anything like this happened to us—well, so what? Never before have we tried to reach the Pole. Damn it, it could happen to anyone headed for the Pole! The ice conditions were lousy? Then tomorrow they'll be better. Terribly cold? We'll get used to it. Things just aren't that bad. Just before drifting off, he resolutely thought to himself that it was necessary to keep on marching toward the Pole even if some of them perished. That was a desperate, evil thought, and, having firmly fixed it in his mind, he understood that everything with him was all right, that his will was not broken.

Climbing out of the tent the morning of March 17, the team noted to their delight that ice conditions had changed for the better. The icefloes had closed ranks; no open water was visible. And the drift during the night, though in fact it had shifted as they had feared, had managed to carry them only a little to the southwest.

Since Vasili was left without skis, Dmitri decided to make his rucksack lighter by distributing part of his load among the others. Melnikov immediately recalled Long Strait, where they had carried the heaviest rucksacks ever, and remarked that "everything comes round again."

Ledenev was quick to correct him. "No," he said, "the ice was worse then, and we had far less experience."

No one had any serious doubts about Dmitri's decision. Without skis, Vasili had to trudge through deep snow, over hummocks and icy ridges. Carrying a rucksack weighing more than twenty-five kilos would have been absolutely impossible.

The team quickly broke camp, got their bearings, and headed northward. They marched fifty minutes, rested ten, and then again hit the road. This was a proven method allowing optimal expenditure of energy and strength. After four such cycles there was a long rest: the tent was set up, a hot meal cooked, and then an hour's nap. They were not making good speed: one of them had no skis, and the rest carried too heavy a load.

All day Dmitri had been thinking of their next radio contact. The fact that a pair of skis had been lost must be admitted, and a new pair dropped by aircraft. He realized that this might occasion undesirable talk on the mainland:

Oh, so these would-be heroes have just set out and already they're asking for help. If news like this reached Moscow, Dmitri knew, some big gun who likes to play it safe might well order the group back to the mainland. Dmitri knew that such a thing could happen. There are always people who find it easier to say no. And this feeling was reinforced by the fact that Henrietta was still so near: just look back and you could see the silent cliffs looming in the distance.

No contact was attempted that day or the next. And no one mentioned anything about it. They all realized that Shparo was biding his time.

Ledenev slapped rigid restrictions on matches: each day he issued only six to the man on KP. It was decided that the most efficient method was to light a candle and use it to light the primus stove. On March 19, while cooking lunch, Vadim ignored this rule and was immediately punished: Ledenev took the treasured box of matches away from him. "We don't trust you with the fire anymore." Davydov did not argue the point.

During these first days they were all tortured by the terrible cold. At times they would joke around just to forget their misery.

"Last night I awoke from the chattering of my own teeth," Melnikov remarked one morning.

"They kept me awake too," Shishkarev parried.

At that point Rakhmanov, who till then had remained almost stubbornly silent, joined the conversation: "I remember a marathon runner giving an interview: 'At first it was awful,' he said, 'but then it got worse and worse.' "

This got them all laughing. They liked the line so much it became a sort of droll refrain that helped them through the worst of it.

Following are some excerpts from the diary of Anatoli Melnikov:

"*March 20.* A cold night, a cold day. My hands freeze

to the radio set. I put the battery by the primus stove to warm it up, and then wrap it in the sleeping bag. All our talk centers around the struggle against the dampness and cold."

"*March 21*. During the night, the cold nearly got us down. The nylon lining of my sleeping bag got to resemble a sheet of tinfoil, and crinkled almost as much. In the morning, we compared notes: who was able to get warm, how they stood up to the cold. Everyone suffered terribly. During the night my nose was frozen, and so was Shparo's ear. Everyone had frostbitten cheeks."

"*March 22*. The sleeping bags are like ice, our down quilts as well. We seem to be freezing into the ice."

The problem was that the severe cold was accompanied by a high level of humidity. Minus thirty-five is not all that cold, but when you're sleeping in wet clothing, in a wet sleeping bag, in a wet tent—well, then it is certainly no bed of roses. The down in the sleeping bags had turned to icy lumps and offered no warmth at all. Zippers on down jackets had frozen, and boots had turned into icy galoshes.

Dmitri sent a dispatch to be published in the paper; it hit us like a gust of frigid air:

"We are concerned over our severe living conditions. Most of all we are oppressed by the cold. During our stops I often think of the fact that ours is the first polar expedition to dispense with fur-lined clothing. Though fur is heavier, it is reliable. But a fur coat will not fit into a rucksack.

"All our warm things are made of down. Always before, we have been quite pleased with them—jackets, sleeping bags, mittens—but now we realize that at this time of year treks across the ocean call for something different.

"In 1970, on one of our very first Arctic treks—on the Taimyr Peninsula—one of the participants, Venyamin

Peskov, trotted around the tent at night in order to get warm. We slept, while he trotted. The temperature then was minus forty-five. I remembered this incident the night of March 20, when all the others were asleep. Even in the sleeping bag my feet were freezing so badly that I climbed out of the tent and began making large circular movements with my legs—first the right and then the left."

In fact, no one slept well that night. They lay around half asleep, shivering from the cold. The only real sleep came during the day, in the hour after lunch. Once there was a long discussion as to how to dry the sleeping bags. Vadim in all seriousness proposed that they dry the bags with the flame from the primus stove: "Put the stove right inside the sleeping bag; that'll dry it fast enough."

"Hah!" snorted Melnikov. "It'll instantly go up in flames."

"It has to be done carefully. With a small flame." Vadim was not giving up. Expecting support, he looked at Dmitri.

"No," said Shparo. "That's no good."

"The sun and the wind are our only hope," Ledenev insisted.

"We must ask for an airdrop—a big piece of polyethylene film," suggested Vasili. "Out of it, we can make a big tent that will hold the heat well. Inside we can light two primus stoves and hang all our belongings up to dry."

It was probably toughest of all on Vasili. After his little swim, his clothing never did dry properly. The third day out he threw away his blue twill trousers, having lost all hope of their ever drying. The thick woolen sweater he wore was also wet, and it was only with great difficulty that he could pull on his boots in the morning. During our midday breaks, while everyone else was resting, Shishkarev trotted around the tent in order to warm his feet. During the night he lay in his sleeping bag thinking: don't forget to wiggle your toes on your left leg, now on your right leg, now check your fingers. He struggled against the cold night and day.

At first he tried to rub his frostbitten cheeks with his mittens, and smeared them with a special cream; but he quickly gave that up.

"Don't worry," Vadim tried to console him. "It'll heal by itself."

All their faces were quickly covered with sores and scabs, but they paid hardly any attention to it.

March 18   To: Shparo

Prefabricated cabin for Sklokin's base camp delivered today by IL-14 from Zhokhov Island to NP-24. While returning to Chersky, approximately 1400 Moscow time (2200 local), tried to spot you in the region of Henrietta, but failed to do so due to darkness. In future, if you hear aircraft above you, send up a flare and go on the air on the USW-band. On March 19 at 1800 (Moscow time) we begin airlifting Sklokin's group from Kotelny to NP-24. Have info on ice conditions along your route from 78° north latitude to NP-24. Can transmit. All the best.

Snegirev, Obukhov

Above is the text of a note airdropped to the skiers. Two days later the following dispatch was radioed to Moscow.

March 20   To: Expedition Headquarters, Moscow

Today the ski group is thirty-five kilometers north of Henrietta Island. Temperature along the route, minus thirty-five. Skis airdropped from IL-14 at 0800 this morning. Sklokin, Ivanov, and part of the cargo moved to NP-24. Radio station of the base group at NP-24 came on the air today at 1250. Tomorrow plan second flight to deliver Shatokhin and rest of cargo to base. Snegirev, Obukhov participating in all operations on IL-14. Their return to Moscow planned for March 22. Operative interaction between the ski team, aircraft, base groups, and airstrips assisted by ham radio operators at Magadan, Tiksi, Chersky, Norilsk, Dickson.

Labutin

Let me flesh out these messages a bit.

After the ski team had started out, Obukhov and I arrived at the settlement of Chersky, base of the air detachment assisting us. Immediately we got down to organizing the base at NP-24. Sklokin's group was still at Kotelny, though according to plan it should already have been on the air from NP-24 and have prepared the first airdrop to the skiers out on the ice.

As representatives of expedition headquarters, we had to undertake several quite complicated flights to resolve this problem. The first one came on Sunday, March 18. From an airstrip near the mouth of the Kolyma, our two-engine IL-14 flew for four hours, raising a flurry of snow behind it as it finally touched down on Zhokhov Island. Here we dug the prefabricated cabin out of the snow and loaded it onto the airplane. Soon we were once again in the air, headed now for NP-24. Two hours to the north we spotted a huge iceberg shaped like a flatiron. On the very edge of that berg, a tiny settlement found shelter: a dozen cabins, a pole flying a red flag, an airstrip.

The aircraft taxied into the "pocket"—a specially cleared area for unloading freight. Coming down the flimsy ladder, we were immediately surrounded by dogs. Oleg, who had never visited a drifting station before, was caught off guard. A bit shaken, he tried to scramble back into the plane. I stopped him: "They don't bite. They're expecting sugar from you." I had learned long ago that these outwardly menacing beasts were in fact very affable and faithful. Dogs are kept at all drifting and coastal polar stations; they warn the men of marauding polar bears and will step boldly into battle, often being mauled, maimed, even killed, for their trouble.

Oleg rummaged in the pockets of his down jacket, found several caramels, and immediately became dog's best friend.

Taking their time, the station crew approached us. It is not customary to make introductions right there at the aircraft—for that there is the lounge in the main cabin, where, in a warm and cozy atmosphere, over a cup of tea, there is plenty of time for talk, both official and unofficial. Almost all the men sported beards. They had lived an entire year on this iceberg in the middle of the Arctic, and just a few weeks remained of their tour of duty. A year of heavy and dangerous work had left its imprint, a certain look of sternness and concentration on their faces.

"Did you bring the mail?" was their first question.

The mail—letters from home, newspapers, magazines—was in the plane. Immediately their faces grew softer, and the creases evened out.

The last to approach us was a black-bearded young man I knew from previous meetings on drifting stations; he was the best cook in the Arctic. For the sake of the ice and the polar night he had given up his position as chef at the fashionable Leningrad restaurant, the Astoria.

"Pasha, good to see you!"

"Hello," came the unenthusiastic reply, as if we had seen each other just yesterday and not three years ago.

"I'm really glad to see you," I said.

But Pasha had no patience with these formalities. "Did you bring any cognac?" he almost demanded.

"What?" I was taken up short.

"The hell with you." Pasha shrugged his shoulders, turned around, and stalked off toward the cabins.

The experience was unsettling. It hadn't occurred to me that a bottle of good cognac might be a welcome gift out here, where there are no cafes or shops.

Only the work at hand rescued me from my suddenly downcast spirits. With the help of the station crew, we quickly off-loaded the prefabricated cabin from the aircraft and tossed the carefully marked parcels onto a tractor-drawn sled that towed us to the station. Tomorrow they would assemble the cabin for Sklokin's group.

The station chief, Igor Popov, was a middle-aged man, friendly enough but a bit phlegmatic. He spoke his words so slowly, dragged them out so much, that it was actually uncomfortable conversing with him. Informed earlier of our basic objectives at NP-24, he invited us to his cabin and asked for further details. Then it suddenly occurred to him that this might be of interest to the entire station. He picked up the intercom. "Radio? Announce over the PA that there will be a general meeting in the main lounge."

Ten minutes later, Oleg and I took turns describing the plan of the expedition. Our hosts listened to us with serious looks on their faces; clearly these were men conversant with the hardships of the higher latitudes. When I announced that Sklokin's group was arriving at the station tomorrow, the men became noticeably more lively. The appearance of new people among an isolated group grown weary of each other's company often introduces a certain element of relaxation, and a welcome change of routine.

"The newcomers go immediately on KP," Popov joked. "That'll be their baptism of fire."

The pilots were already glancing at us impatiently: it was time to return to Chersky. We quickly discussed all the questions about accommodating Sklokin's group and, saying goodbye, promised to fly the others in tomorrow. The IL-14 took off and headed for the mainland.

The navigator drew a line on the map from the NP-24 to Chersky—a distance of fourteen hundred kilometers. I took a closer look at the map: the line passed within a centimeter of Henrietta Island.

"How about a slight detour, Commander? Let's take a look at our boys from the air."

The pilot made some calculations with his slide rule. "It'll be dark," he replied, a note of hesitation in his voice; "we won't see a thing."

"They'll hear our engines, switch on their radio, and make contact. Then they'll shoot up a flare. Let's give it a try."

The commander too wanted to see the skiers on the ocean ice. He hesitated for a split second, then nodded his head: "Okay. We'll look for them for fifteen minutes, tops, then we leave. Our fuel is limited."

Two hours later—it was night, and the aircraft was flying through the dark by instruments—the pilot called me into his cockpit. He pointed straight ahead: "Henrietta."

In the dark you could barely make out the glacier and the snow-covered cliffs. I suggested we fly straight to the island, then veer a hundred and eighty degrees and begin tacking for a distance of thirty to forty kilometers. The pilot agreed, and for fifteen minutes the IL-14 conscientiously zigzagged through the night sky. We all looked down hoping to see the spark of a flare or a signal fire; the radio operator was all ears on the USW-band. But there was no response. Below us the night was pitch black.

On March 19, at 2330, having barely recuperated from fifteen hours of flying, we again took off from Chersky. Four hours later we landed on Kotelny, where Sklokin's group awaited us. Fyodor told us that Shparo had asked us to drop a pair of skis and some matches—they had just received his radiogram. We decided to fly to NP-24, unload Sklokin and Ivanov with their cargo, and then fly to

Henrietta and locate the skiers. After making the drop, we would return to Kotelny for Shatokhin and the remainder of the cargo. In addition to this second trip, two more would be necessary: we had to deliver to the drifting station a supply of gasoline for future flights to the ski team. Barring bad weather, these operations should take up no more than two days.

But the commander of the aircraft, our old friend Oleg Okhonsky, was in his usual pessimistic frame of mind. "When did you ever see good weather in these parts?" he groaned. "It'll take at least a week."

But for some reason I thought we would be lucky.

On March 20, at 0600 hours, we were at NP-24; half an hour later we took off for Henrietta. We were in a hurry for a very obvious reason: we wanted to reach the area the ski group was in while we still had some daylight.

On a sheet of paper, Okhonsky traced a complex and quite ingenious pattern for the search. The crew was nervous, and the commander, though he tried to calm everyone, was no less so than the rest. To find a small group of people among the icy hummocks—this was a problem they had never come up against.

At 0830 hours, as we approached Henrietta, Okhonsky went into a steep turn, headed back to where we had come from, banking slightly eastwards, and began the search. Five minutes later the commander heard in his earphones a faint signal from the ski team; a few minutes more and their words could be made out. Soon after, off the starboard engine, we saw a spurt of orange smoke. Okhonsky descended to twenty meters, and in three passes we successfully dropped the skis, the matches, and my note. At 0855 hours the plane set out for Kotelny, and three hours later made a safe landing alongside the by now familiar cabins at Temp Bay.

The crew needed a rest. The next flight was scheduled for twelve hours later, actually on March 21. The pilots had their evening meal, watched an old movie in the canteen, and went off to sleep. I radioed Labutin (who some thirty kilometers from here was monitoring the airwaves round the clock), got the latest news from him, and eagerly followed the pilots' example.

Oleg and I were really fatigued by the long flights. Over the past five days we had spent practically fifty hours shuttling around in the air between NP-24, Kotelny Island, and the settlement of Chersky. The next day it was more of the same: the din of snowmobiles and aircraft engines; loading the plane with cargo and gasoline drums; snoozing in the air above the endless fields of ice. Kotelny, NP-24; NP-24, Kotelny.

It seemed to go on forever. . . .

Sklokin's transmitter at NP-24 first came on the air on March 21. On the same day I had my first radio conversation with Shparo since the ski team's start. This is how it went.

At 1255 Moscow time (well past midnight at NP-24), Sklokin's group along with Obukhov and myself met in their cabin. Ivanov made a few abracadabra gestures at the radio station and switched on the loudspeaker: out of it came the clear voice of Dmitri Shparo:

"This is U-Zero-K." These were the call letters of the ski team's transmitter.

"Good evening," came the reply from Labutin on Kotelny. "This is U-Zero-PR listening to you very attentively."

"Hello, Lenya." One could easily make out the weariness in Dmitri's voice. "Our weather here today has taken a turn for the worse. No sun. Strong winds." Here he heaved a deep sigh. "We were unable to get our bearings. I would say the group's position is the following: twenty degrees from Henrietta's meridian to the northeast; distance from the island, approximately fifty kilometers."

"Roger."

"Any other questions? I want to speak to Fyodor at NP-24. Fyodor, can you hear me?"

Georgi moved the mike over in front of Sklokin.

"Good evening, Dmitri. I read you loud and clear."

"Here's what I want to know. Can you tell us what direction NP-24 has been drifting the past few days? We need to know in order to pinpoint our position and choose the correct course. It's possible our group and the station are in one and the same ice mass."

"Got it. I'll check that out right away."

"Dmitri," I said, "Hello. Do you recognize my voice?"

"Not right off. Is that you, Vladimir?"

"Sure it's me. Good evening!"

"Hi there! I thought you'd already be in Moscow. It's great you're here. How's it going?"

"Everything normal. All the equipment for Sklokin's group has been airlifted to NP-24. From Temp we're now flying in fuel for future flights. We'll wrap up everything by tomorrow, and Oleg and I will fly to Moscow."

"Got it. Very good."

"Dmitri, remember: orange smoke is seen very poorly from the air. In an air search the main emphasis should be on the radio beacon."

"Roger. What else?"

"When we dropped the skis, at what distance did you first see and hear our aircraft?"

"First, we saw you; then we heard you. From Henrietta you headed straight for us. We spotted you at about twenty kilometers."

"Got it. Another question: do you need data on ice conditions along meridian 156 from 75 degrees latitude?"

"Shoot—I've got a pencil here."

"Ice conditions similar to those we observed yesterday from the air in the region of the group stretch out to the north for ten kilometers. Then comes an area of fresh hummocks, including a strip of sludge ice five hundred meters wide. Some sixty-five to seventy kilometers north of Henrietta there will be comparatively smooth pack ice. There are few ridges, especially to the north."

"And the conditions are like that all the way to NP-24?"

"Approximately. I would say the hummocking rates one to two points. No patches of open water visible."

"That's clear, and thanks. Can we count on an ice reconnaissance report along meridian 158?"

"Tomorrow we fly back to the mainland; I'll ask the pilots to make a detour through that area."

"You can probably guess what's worrying all of us." Here Dmitri made a long pause. I waited patiently, knowing his habit of weighing every word before speaking. "In all likelihood we won't be dropping in to NP-24. You got that?"

"I believe you'll be doing the right thing. I think the station is drifting north-northwest. I think given our main objective, your visit here is not obligatory."

"The benefits of a visit are clear, but the drawbacks outweigh them. Right?"

"As I understand it, your decision on this has already been made. You have obviously veered away from us to the east. Any visit to NP-24 is out of the question."

"We are acting with the schedule in mind."

Our conversation ended on that note, as Fyodor had returned with the data on the station's drift. It was astounding: NP-24 was now drifting southwest, and had been for the past few days. Rather timidly, Fyodor gave Dmitri this information. Shparo could not believe his ears, and asked that it be repeated. Sklokin obliged. After a long period of silence, Dmitri said his goodbyes, making no comment on this unexpected bit of news.

March 22. Having completed our work, Oleg and I board a regular Aeroflot flight and take off for Moscow.

On Skis to the North Pole!

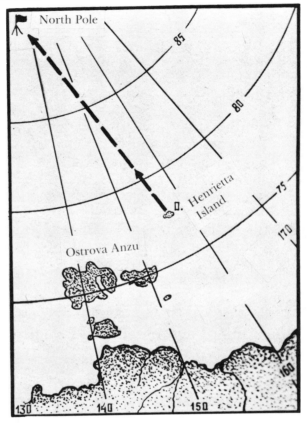

Members of the expedition, working at the bases (from left): Mikhael Deyev, Leonid Labutin, Georgii Ivanov, Alexander Shatokhin, and Fyodor Sklokin, chief of base group SP-24.

Kotelnoy Island. Base radiostation for the expedition.

110

Senior radioman Leonid Labutin receives trans-
mission at base from the seven at the
North Pole.

The expedition's chronometers.

Dividing up crackers and chocolate was hard. Yuri Khmelevsky
is in charge of scientific expedition today.

Doctor Vadim Davydov

Vladimir Rakhmanov

Vladimir Ledenev

Anatoli Melnikov can reach the whole world from his tent.

Expedition chief Dmitri Shparo.

Vasili Shishkarev's pack weighs close to 50 kg.

Before setting off on Henrietta Island.

Henrietta Island

Which way?

The explorer's home—a tent.

After putting together his parachute, Yuri Khmelevsky has to divide
up goodies for the backpacks.

Pitching a tent during a blizzard. . . .

On thin ice.

Falls like this were daily occurrences—and dangerous.

Light and heat.

The ice is at least 4 m thick here.

Aerial view of expedition camp.

A plane came over the camp four times dropping supplies.

White desert.

Burning garbage.

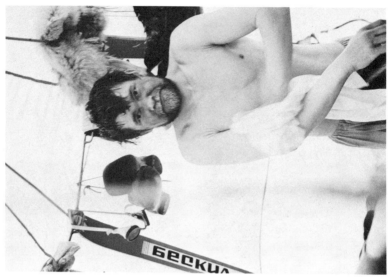

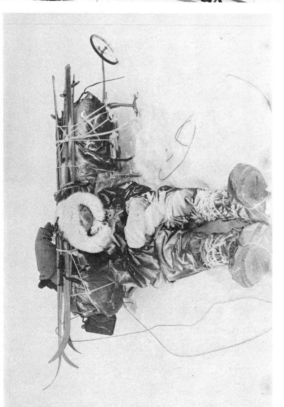

Taking a break. . . .

Steambath at the 88th parallel.

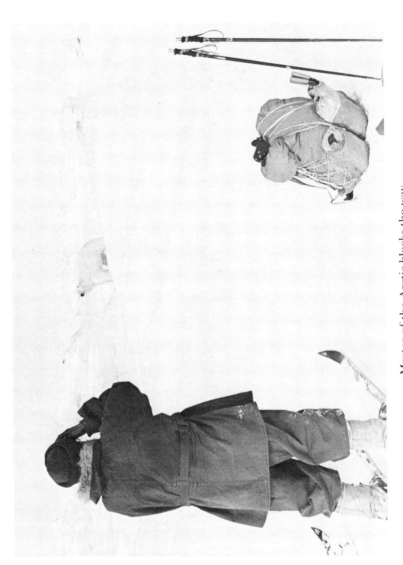

Master of the Arctic blocks the way.

Trying to float. . . .

At the North Pole.

126

Tired but exultant . . . at the top of the planet Earth.

Raising the flag at the North Pole. There are pictures of famous Russians explorers E.V. Toll, V.A. Rusanov, and G. Ya. Sedov.

February 1980, London's Sir Stanley Royce and D. Shparo.

The seven in London (February 1980) for the first press conference.

Up the Down Escalator

Oh, those first weeks back in Moscow. For me, the days and nights were one long blur. Telephone calls and radiograms around the clock, never-ending reports to my superiors, articles for the newspaper and for radio, memorandums, weather reports, meetings at headquarters —there seemed no end to it.

At first, there was no getting rid of ham radio operators. Everyone who had managed to make contact with Labutin, or had even heard his voice on the air, considered it his duty to inform me about it, to say "Everything is okay with Leonid." I could not quite bring myself to scolding them for waking me up at all hours of the night with their calls; they were certainly motivated by good intentions. At times, however—especially in the wee hours of the morning—it was all I could do to keep from exploding at such importunate concern. Gradually I managed to convince my new friends that, first of all, I myself made radio contact with Labutin daily and for long periods, and, second of all, besides myself there were others in Moscow who would indeed be only too pleased to get such calls at home at five in the morning. Then I would give them the telephone number of Alexander Tenyakshev, who was now our Moscow radio operator, or of the expedition's chief geographer and archivist, Alexander Shumilov, who during those days was busy preparing a series of TV travelogues. Sometimes, however, my little practical joke would boomerang.

One morning at six, a call from Vnukovo Airport outside Moscow got me out of bed: "Hello, is that *Komsomolskaya Pravda*?"

"Yes, you're almost right." I did not want to waste time explaining the difference between my apartment and the editorial offices.

"Your film has arrived at the airport," said a wheezy male voice.

"What film, what the. . .?" I began to boil, but realizing that this film from the Arctic was intended for television, decided to spoil the night for Shumilov as well.

"You know," said I, "at *Komsomolskaya Pravda* there's another telephone, where they're sitting and waiting for this film. Dial this number. . ." and I gave Shumilov's number.

No sooner had my head touched the pillow than I was out like a light. But some ten minutes later the pre-dawn silence was shattered by the ringing telephone: "The film has arrived!" exclaimed the happy voice of Shumilov.

There were, of course, tears as well as laughter.

For me at that time, humankind fell into two halves. In one camp were those who wholeheartedly accepted the expedition, who anxiously followed its northward progress. In the other camp were those who, consumed by their own envy or gnawed at by some inferiority complex, thought that in the atomic age there was no need to ski across icy oceans, who believed that the underlying motive of our undertaking was simply to attain fame and glory.

One such sourpuss grabbed me by the lapel one day in the hallway outside our office.

"Well," he said, "do you think our heroes will reach the Pole?"

"Of course they will." I didn't quite yet understand what he was driving at.

"For a million I too would make it," he snorted, with obvious cynicism. "Your expedition did cost a million, didn't it?"

What could I say? Though I certainly didn't feel like providing apologetics for the expedition, I did try to explain to this character that the funds spent on the expedition did not exceed the sums commonly spent on stamp collectors' conferences and the like; that the members of the expedition received nothing but traveling expenses; and that the moral gain from this epic could not be measured in money.

But he was inexorable. "Do you think Shparo will be decorated with an Order of Lenin if he makes it to the Pole? What kind of medal do you think? They probably won't give him the highest award."

Those days I stood practically defenseless against such remarks. I simply had no strength to shrug them off as jokes, or to seriously uphold my point of view.

But for the record it must be said that there were not really so many ill-wishers. And they certainly did not determine the mood of those days. Both in the USSR and abroad a lively and sincere interest prevailed toward the North Pole ski trek. All the major world news agencies reported the group's progress regularly, and items on the expedition were carried in all major newspapers. The latest news from the Arctic was regularly broadcast on radio and television.

The first meeting of expedition headquarters after the start was held on March 30. The atmosphere of that meeting very accurately reflected the situation during those days.

Standing in front of a map of the Arctic basin, I gave a brief summary of the early stages of the expedition. I went into details about the difficulties of the prestart period, about the organization of the base camps, about the group's departure from Henrietta Island.

"Getting out onto the ice was not easy; I might even say it was dramatic. The team had to pay a very heavy price for the first few meters. Two of the group broke through the ice. But there is no cause for alarm; the group is now back on schedule, covering on the average twenty kilometers a day. Ice conditions are normal. However, I do not wish to appear overoptimistic. Abnormally low temperatures are prevailing in that region of the Arctic. For quite some time the thermometer has hovered around minus thirty-five."

I looked up at the clock.

"I would like to remind you that today—to be precise, in some fifteen minutes—the first airdrop of food and fuel is to be made to the group at its camp on the ice."

At this point the Deputy Editor-in-Chief of the paper, Boris Mokrousov, asked if there were any questions. With none immediately forthcoming, he asked one of his own: "Could you give us some details of the start from Henrietta Island?"

I turned to the map behind me, disturbed at the turn things were taking. Some of those present—I could see by their faces—were dissatisfied because the group was unable to keep out of danger even on the first day out. What they really wanted, of course, was a red carpet rolled all the way to the North Pole.

"The difficulty was that at the shoreline the skiers encountered a wall of ice dropping precipitously into

132

either open water or fast-flowing sludge ice. The most important thing here was to choose the right moment to cross, and such a moment was chosen. The group operated smoothly, and things went without a hitch."

After mouthing a few more such cautious phrases, I wanted to steer things away from the subject of the hazardous start, but then, just when I thought I had, Oleg Obukhov, unaware of the mounting hostility, began to speak, vividly expatiating on the rigors and perils of the start.

And then, to my great chagrin, Oleg was being interrupted by the one man in the room I least wanted to hear from. "Allow me to speak!" the man said. "Allow me to express myself on this subject. I cannot imagine any justification for taking such risks at the very start of the expedition. You might have sent the entire expedition to its death! The group should have hopped over that area by helicopter. Hopped over!"

He emphasized these words, holding an index finger aloft and looking out at us over his eyeglasses.

"That option was unacceptable." I could not control myself.

"Just a minute, please." His finger was now pointed directly at me. "You, if I may be allowed to say so, represented headquarters at the start. And that means that it was precisely you who placed the expedition in jeopardy. Or do you not consider yourself responsible to the people in this room?" At this point he cast his gaze left and right, attempting eye contact with everyone present. Are we or are we not headquarters? he seemed to be asking.

They all seemed to avert their eyes at this, and began shuffling the documents in front of them. This was a crucial moment. If this man was supported by others, the consequences could be very serious indeed. Any future situation that might imperil the ski team would give head-

133

quarters the pretext they needed for resorting to the most drastic and unfounded measures.

"I would like to remind you," Obukhov interjected, "that there was a helicopter on the island providing back-up."

"If anyone went to the bottom, the helicopter could hardly have helped," our opponent trumpeted. "That's the Arctic, and there is no joking around with the Arctic."

"Words of gold," I found myself saying. I had not really meant to say this aloud, but having done so decided to go on: "I might add that they are words often spoken by the chief of this expedition, Dmitri Shparo, who, unlike the lot of us here, has covered hundreds of kilometers across Arctic icefloes. Believe me, he knows his business."

No one else ventured an opinion, and I realized we had got the upper hand. Later it was decided to try to plot the group's future movements, to pinpoint on the map the anticipated airdrops—in short, to draw up a tentative long-range timetable. The chief of the North Coast Route Administration, Kirill Chubakov (who two years earlier had been one of the leaders of the polar expedition of the atomic icebreaker *Arktika*) argued that a comparison between such a timetable and the actual progress of the group would enable the headquarters to better evaluate any future situation. He also asked that Shparo be reminded, during the next radio contact, of the need to record observations of the weather, ice conditions, drift, and snow covering.

"These observations may come in handy for planning voyages along the North Coast Route," Chubakov went on. "I would also like to draw your attention to the fact that soon the group will be passing over the underwater Lomonosov Range. This region is very tricky—active hummocking, icefloes in rapid motion, vast expanses of open water. The group must be very careful, and must be prepared for some surprises."

The next speaker was Mikhail Novikov, representing the medical sciences at headquarters.

"The director of our institute, Academician Gazenko, has suggested organizing a special first-aid and resuscitation team for monitoring the expedition. The group is to include a number of specialists who attend cosmonauts upon their return from space.

"There is no need, my friends, to fear the word *resuscitation*. However, one must bear in mind that anything can happen in real life, and that, if need be, this well-equipped team is ready to fly out to the North to provide immediate aid to any who may need it."

Another Deputy Editor-in-Chief of *Komsomolskaya Pravda*, Valeri Kisilev, took this opportunity to interject a few remarks bearing on the health of the skiers. "I have a very interesting bit of information," he said in a low tone and coughing just a bit. "A few days ago, the members of the expedition talked by radio with their wives. In the opinion of the wives, everything with their men is going fine—their voices are cheerful, their intonations clear. This, I think, is indicative."

"Yes, these are important indications," agreed Novikov. "In such situations a wife can often detect a false note that might otherwise escape observation." He then turned to me: "What are the possibilities that the ski team will visit NP-24?"

For the second time that day I was feeling uncomfortable. Novikov had asked his question because he, as a scientist and the representative of the institute whose medical research program the expedition was cooperating in, wanted to intercept the group in mid-trek, to perform comprehensive intermediate investigations, and to assess the health of each participant at the one-third mark. I understood Novikov's desires, and sympathized with them, but realized more clearly than anyone present that the ski team's route would take them far from NP-24. I hesitated to bring this up, however, for fear of inciting the opposition once again. I was in a quandary as to what to say when seemingly out of nowhere I was saved by Chubakov.

"I would not recommend that the group visit NP-24," he said. "The skiers are now on a more favorably drifting ice field, and there is little sense in their deviating to the west. A visit to the station would put them behind schedule. Perhaps, if headquarters supports me, we might officially notify Shparo of our recommendation."

Novikov, who had had plenty of experience in such discussions, instantly realized that it was senseless to argue the point. "I by no means insist that the group visit the station," he said. "But isn't there some possibility that a limited number of people, perhaps using a helicopter, could visit the group somewhere along its route?"

"That would require a rather large and costly operation," I explained. "I doubt your institute would agree to finance it."

"I don't think we should rule out Novikov's proposal just yet," Mokrousov interceded. "All the pros and cons must be weighed thoroughly and everything taken into account."

I could have kicked myself at this point; Mokrousov's words made much better sense than my own. Everyone seemed quite satisfied to table the suggestion. Novikov then recommended that we keep closer watch on the health of Vasili Shishkarev, and asked that he not be overloaded with work. Finally Mokrousov summarized the discussion, and the meeting was adjourned. Everything had ended very positively.

Meanwhile, out on the polar ice, the ski team persevered. Following are a few extracts from the diary of Vladimir Ledenev.

"*March 24.* Woke up at 0340 hours. I'm on duty today.

Fired up the primus stove, climbed out of the tent, and quickly got warm. Our moist clothing is our main discomfort.

"We must get used to this lifestyle. Not to fight the cold, but to reach a point where you no longer notice it. All of us are pretty well frostbitten. Anatoli and I are coughing. My pulse rate is high—70–80 beats per minute, sometimes 100. I hope I don't fall sick.

"*March 26*. Today was probably the toughest day of all. We hit the road at 0815 hours. The weather was cold but sunny; however, by the end of our first stop the sky had clouded over. Visibility dropped drastically. Moreover, we entered a zone of badly chewed-up ice.

"After our fifth stop we had a cold lunch: sausage, salt pork, sugar, soda biscuits, hardtack. We did not set up the tent or light up the primus stove. After lunch we went on for another four hours. Really exhausted. Wanted to drink very much. In the evening we quickly pitched camp and with great relish gulped down the supper Vasili had cooked.

"We have been informed by radio that on March 30 the plane will make the first drop of food and gasoline.

"*March 28*. We spent the whole day clambering over ridges of hummocks, each new ridge worse than the last. In one spot, the thick pack ice had been ruptured, forming a deep ice canyon directly in our path. We advanced some one and a half kilometers into this canyon before finding ourselves in a deadend. On three sides we were surrounded by walls of ice some ten meters high. It was clear as day we could not go any further."

Take note of this last entry. Having made it the evening of March 28, Ledenev put away his diary and drifted off to sleep with the others. They had set up on the canyon floor right where they were, having decided their problem was best slept on. This turned out to be a very wise decision. When they awoke the next morning the

137

drift had rotated the icefloe so that the only way out led exactly where they wanted to go—due north. In those few hours ice conditions had changed beyond recognition: the ridges seemed lower, and valleys and canyons had formed between them. The Arctic had presented them yet another surprise, this time a rather pleasant one.

But a far less welcome surprise, much more unexpected, had slowly been unfolding, and could no longer be ignored: a head-on drift was definitely carrying the ice they stood on in the opposite direction of the Pole. In one of his radio messages Dmitri described their progress as "going up the down escalator."

To understand the full impact of this situation, a little background is in order.

The reader may wonder why Henrietta Island, which is fifteen hundred kilometers from the Pole, was chosen as the jumping-off point. Why not Severnaya Zemlya, a mere thousand kilometers from the Pole, or Franz Josef Land, even closer? The fact is that we had to trust the staff of the Arctic and Antarctic Institute, who after all had studied for some time the regularities of polar ice movement. According to them, the general drift in the eastern sector of the Arctic Ocean, along Henrietta's meridian, has a pronounced northward trend. It was felt that the natural drift of the ice fields here could save the ski team up to two hundred kilometers. Had they started from Franz Josef Land or Severnaya Zemlya, they would have had to "row against the current," as observations over many years had detected a steady southwestward drift in this sector that would add approximately three hundred kilometers to the trip. Moreover, hummocking is encountered here much more often. So, everything considered, it seemed wisest for the team to take the longer route, in the confident expectation that the drift would be on their side.

Imagine then Dmitri's amazement when Sklokin informed him on the twenty-first that NP-24 was drifting to the southwest. Well how do you like that, he must have thought; if the station is drifting in the same ice mass we are, then we too are being carried to the south.

Up the down escalator.

Even before Sklokin's revelation, they had half suspected something of the sort. But it was hard even to conceive of its happening. When Henrietta Island was still within their range of vision, Rakhmanov had taken azimuth readings in the evening, and had repeated the procedure the next morning. Comparing the findings, he had been astounded: during the night they had been carried back approximately two kilometers to the southwest. Initially, because of the difficulties of the first few days, there had not really been time to give much thought to the matter; they simply considered it a brief whim of the drift, a freak occurrence. But gradually they began to notice that a general head-on drift was robbing them of as much as six kilometers a day.

"What treachery!" exclaimed Dmitri.

"Treachery?" Yuri did not agree. "Here we must be ready for anything."

"Yes, but must we get *every*thing, and right at the start, too?" interjected Melnikov. "A dip in ice-cold water, skis at the bottom of the ocean, bitter cold, this head-on drift. . . ."

This conversation took place the evening of March 28, in a tent illuminated by the dim light of a single candle. Dmitri was trying to finish his dispatch for *Komsomolskaya Pravda*. Rakhmanov was busy cooking supper, which as usual consisted of oatmeal with big chunks of butter and dehydrated meat, biscuits, salt pork, chocolate, and strong coffee. Melnikov was checking the antenna, preparing to go on the air.

The rest had crawled into their sleeping bags and were delighting in the warmth. Someone was actually snoring.

139

"Come and get it!" called Rakhmanov, removing the pot of oatmeal from the primus stove. "Give me your bowls."

All of a sudden it became quite lively in the tent, metal bowls clanking against each other and good-natured jokes flying through the air.

"Anatoli, watch out your spoon doesn't freeze to your tongue."

"Did you notice how Vadim's eyes light up when he sees food? He makes it twice as bright in here."

Actually, there was a good deal of truth in these humorous remarks. There really were times when spoons had frozen to their lips, and the sight of food would light up the eyes of any one of them. For no matter how nourishing their rations were, the skiers expended so much energy that the feeling of hunger seemed never to leave them.

Melnikov was particularly fond of tasty food, and of eating his fill of it, too. But no sooner had he picked up his spoon than Labutin's voice came over the radio.

"My food is getting cold," Melnikov moaned; but he picked up the microphone nonetheless. For him the radio was something sacred.

He informed the base camp of their coordinates, received the weather forecast for the coming day, and only then asked Labutin to call back in half an hour so he could eat his supper.

"Okay," agreed Labutin, adding with a laugh: "that is, if a bear doesn't get us in the meantime."

Melnikov was already bolting down his supper and paid no attention to the remark. But things were happening on Kotelny—Labutin was not just kidding. Even as he spoke, a polar bear was paying them a visit. The dogs, of whom it is said they fear nothing—not even the devil, not to mention a bear—went scurrying away, tails between their legs, the moment they spotted him. Taking

140

his time, their guest inspected the base, sniffed around the snowmobile and the tractor, lingered awhile at the garbage dump—in short, behaved as if he owned the place.

Labutin was sitting by the radio in the main building, having spoken to Melnikov, Deyev was at the controls of the transmitter in a small trailer about a hundred meters off. Suddenly Labutin was speaking to him over the intercom: "Don't go outside under any circumstances. And lock the door."

"Why?" Deyev asked. Was this some kind of joke?

"A bear. . . ." Labutin managed to say, but just then they were disconnected.

Leonid looked out the window. The bear had climbed a snowdrift to the roof of the van, and had snapped the intercom wire. Labutin clapped his hands to his head. If that bear gets to the other wires, he thought, there's going to be trouble: he'll take out the whole long distance communications system. And in thirty minutes I have to resume contact with the ski team. Labutin armed himself with a flare gun and with everyone else in the room ran outside. He began firing flares in the direction of the bear. Burning balls of fire, sizzling and crackling, fell all around the beast, but failed to impress. At last the bear sauntered down from the roof, and with a great sense of personal dignity made his exit. (Several hours later he made another raid, this time behaving much more aggressively. The dogs whined pitifully and begged to be let indoors, something that had never happened before.)

Meanwhile, out on the ice, the team, snuggled comfortably in their sleeping bags, had finished supper. All of them, feeling warm and full and very, very tired, had drifted off—all, that is, but Shparo and Melnikov, who had still to send their dispatch. Every day, it seemed, they lost an hour or more of sleep dealing with the radio.

Then Dmitri took the mike: "Leonid, are you ready to record my dispatch?"

"Sure thing. The tape recorder's going."

"The headline is the following: At the 80th Parallel. Here comes the text: I had a dream. No, I dreamed not of lilacs, nor of the rain in May, not even of the caressing waves of the Black Sea. Instead I dreamed of ice, grey and very recent. Along it a terrifying wave was rushing, but without breaking the crust. A helicopter hovered over our heads. They were planning to drop seven rucksacks to us. They tried to drive into my head the idea that these rucksacks were absolutely necessary, but I was thinking of something else: how were we going to carry all this stuff? Must each man lug two rucksacks?

"Nearby, Melnikov was tossing in his sleep; he too was dreaming of something. He kept muttering: 'Take my radiogram, take my radiogram. . . .'

"In the morning, Vadim Davydov was indignant: why did Vasili make him try on twelve pairs of mittens one after the other? Also a dream.

"These dreams were a reflection of our anxiety over our severe living conditions. We were oppressed by the cold."

Outside the tent the blue twilight turned indigo. Night was about to fall on the huge expanses of the Arctic Ocean. On all sides the tent was surrounded by the foreboding jagged teeth of icy hummocks.

Melnikov was fighting to stay awake at the radio. Feeling a bit irritated, he reflected as to how there was too much lyricism in Dmitri's dispatches—he might have made them shorter. He thought of how he could avoid freezing tonight. How he had to put up with the batteries in his sleeping bag to protect them from the cold. He thought of how nice it would be to nibble on a chocolate bar now. . . . His thoughts crawled one on top of another, becoming confused, breaking up. . . . He got warmer next to Shparo's shoulder. It felt good, he was almost asleep. . . .

"March 26." Shparo mumbled on in a monotonous

142

tone. "We had planned nine fifty-minute jaunts instead of eight. On recent days the sun has been shining, and we have traveled across large expanses of old ice. Then all of a sudden the Arctic hit us with everything: clouds came in from the east, the wind came howling, the air around us was filled with a white mist. And that was not all. The pack ice ended, and we stepped onto ice perhaps a year old, terribly broken up in every direction. Fresh hummocks stood out in blue silhouette against the white. All the way to the horizon, the Arctic resembled a gigantic stone quarry: grottoes, ravines, labyrinths. Blazing the trail out in front were Ledenev and Shishkarev."

Silence filled the tent. Everyone was asleep. Radio contact was over. Dmitri and Anatoli, not wasting a single second, crawled into their sleeping bags. Tomorrow was going to be a tough day. The flame of the candle flickered out, and for hundreds of kilometers around not a single light shone. Only the dark blue polar night.

March 30. On the fifteenth day of their trek, the plan called for an airdrop of food and gasoline to the ice camp.

The day was sunny and windy. Temperature, minus thirty. Until lunch the group moved at its regular pace. Then, shortly after noon, having completed five legs, they pitched camp before a ridge of hummocks, set up the radio equipment, and got ready to receive the aircraft. Everyone was in very good spirits; they had two days of rest ahead of them. They could dry their clothing, have a good sleep, lick their wounds, eat their fill—or almost, at any rate. After two weeks of continuous drudgery, all this was regarded as the greatest of joys.

Khmelevsky and Rakhmanov pinpointed their position: 79°09' north latitude, 156° east longitude.

"If it weren't for that damned southern drift, we'd already be at the 80th parallel," Rakhmanov complained.

Yuri said nothing. Once again he was immersed in his favorite state, observing himself and others as if from

143

the sidelines. This was almost a kind of split personality. One Khmelevsky was engaged in the world—working with others, suffering and struggling—while another Khmelevsky observed all this from afar, from a sort of lofty philosophical pinnacle. Yuri prized this state, and never passed up a chance to immerse himself in it.

Even now, oblivious to the minus-thirty temperature and the razor-sharp wind, he took his time constructing a framework of skis and hanging his sleeping bag on it to dry. Deep inside, he was trying to determine whether the desired split had occurred or not.

Shiskarev was helping Melnikov set up the antenna with the aid of ski poles. As usual, this took but a few minutes, and soon Anatoli had made radio contact with Kotelny and NP-24. He reported their coordinates and local weather conditions, and asked when they could expect the plane. From NP-24 Sklokin replied that the IL-14 was there already, and was prepared to take off.

"We were just waiting for your final coordinates," came Fyodor's voice. "They're on their way."

Anatoli asked Labutin and Sklokin to keep their receivers tuned to that frequency; then from his rucksack he pulled out a metal box containing a medium-wave radio beacon that would serve as a homing device. This was an invention of Labutin's. At a distance of a hundred kilometers the aircraft zeroes in on the signal and a radio compass guides it directly to the team's position. That was how it worked, in theory at least, and also in tests conducted on the mainland. Today, however, things would not go so smoothly. Today the radio beacon refused to function and there seemed no possibility of repairing it.

Anatoli looked at his watch. Ten minutes ago the plane had taken off from NP-24 and was headed in their direction. Soon the radio operator on board would be expecting their signal.

Melnikov lunged toward the radio. In a tension-filled

144

voice, he called NP-24. Georgi Ivanov answered immediately. At that momeent Sklokin was up in the IL-14, going along as supervisor of the airdrop.

"Georgi," instructed Melnikov, in a tone intentionally kept calm, "inform them on board the plane that they should not count on the beacon. It's on the fritz. Do you read me?"

"Perfectly—the radio beacon is on the fritz. Anything else?"

"Tell them to enter the region of our coordinates, and to then start searching for the group according to the standard pattern. When we hear their engines, we'll switch on the USW-band and try to make contact."

All seven of them were by this time in the tent. No one made any comment; as usual, they waited for Shparo to speak.

Dmitri did not look particularly concerned. He simply reminded them that four parachutes would be dropped over the camp. He emphasized that the wind might drag the containers and parachutes quite far after they came down.

"That is why someone must be responsible for each parachute. Rakhmanov and Khmelevsky will look after the first one, Shishkarev and Ledenev the second one. . . ."

Dmitri gave all these orders as if he did not doubt for a second that the plane would find their tiny tent amid all the snow and ice.

"It's time," Melnikov declared. "According to schedule, the IL-14 should already be in our area."

Armed with flares and smoke signals the team emerged from the tent. Almost instantly they spotted the plane, approaching them from the northwest.

Vasili switched on the USW radio slung over his shoulder: "Aircraft this is Ice Group. Can you read me?"

"Loud and clear," replied the pilot. "Only we can't see you. Tell us where to fly."

145

"Turn a bit left and in a minute or so you'll be passing over our tent."

"Roger—a bit left."

The aircraft banked and was now very close to the camp. The smoke signals were set off, and the IL-14 waved its wings to confirm that the group had been spotted. The plane zoomed over the tent and immediately went into a steep turn so as to make another pass.

The first parachute came down quite far away—three hundred meters or so—and Yuri and Vladimir set out at a trot toward it. But there was no trouble with the next three: they came down right in the camp. Vasili thanked the pilots over the radio, and the aircraft headed back to NP-24.

The entire operation had gone off brilliantly—a veritable holiday on ice. Next to the tent the men were eagerly unpacking the containers. There was food for their two-day bivouac, rations for the next fifteen days' travel, new batteries, signal devices, letters, newspapers, jerry cans of fuel. Plenty of gasoline had been dropped—an entire sixty liters—so they would not have to economize while they were resting, so they could dry their belongings thoroughly. The last few drops of the old stock of fuel had been used up that morning.

Ledenev enthusiastically tackled the primus stoves. He filled them, pumped them properly, opened the valves, and applied a lighted match. Both stoves—they were foolproof Febus stoves from Austria—all of a sudden sputtered and coughed, bellowed out black soot, and then stopped burning altogether. "What the devil," muttered Ledenev under his breath. "It must be the fuel injector." He began cleaning the fuel injectors and asked Vasili to fuel up the new Soviet primus stove, the Bumblebee that had just been dropped to them, and to light it up.

Another attempt was made to light up the Febus stoves but to no avail. Vasili's Bumblebee also refused to work. By now Ledenev was darker than a thundercloud. It seems he knew what was wrong.

"Vasili, listen to me. Only be quiet and don't panic. We'll never be able to light up these stoves."

"Why?" Shishkarev's eyes widened.

"Come closer. What I tell you now need not be known immediately to all the rest. The jerry cans contain not gasoline. . . ."

"Solar oil!" exclaimed Vasili. "Diesel fuel!"

Nearby, five of their comrades, in a carefree and happy mood, were piling up the gifts that had dropped from the sky, anticipating with pleasure two entire days of warmth and rest.

This might be a good place to tell you a little more about our friend Vladimir Ledenev and how he came to join the expedition. Strolling along Mir Avenue August 19, 1971, he came across a fresh issue of *Komsomolskaya Pravda* pinned up on a sidewalk bulletin board. In it he read an account of one of the first polar expeditions organized by Dmitri Shparo, and immediately forgot where he was going and what he was doing. He sat down on a nearby park bench, thought awhile, then got up and walked briskly to our editorial offices. Half an hour later, on the sixth floor of our offices on Pravda Street, I first set eyes on Vladimir Ledenev.

"I wish to participate in the expedition to the Pole," he declared, hardly having introduced himself.

"But so far no one has mentioned the Pole. Why do you think such an expedition is being prepared?"

"I am sure of it," he said, looking me directly in the eyes.

"If you want to work in our expedition, then you surely must realize the difficulties that are in store."

Ledenev winced and seemed, if this was possible, to become even more serious than before. The question could not be resolved here and now, he said and time was being wasted on unnecessary discussions. "I'm not afraid of difficulties," he said.

"I suppose not. But you can't just walk in and join the expedition. You have to earn the right."

"What do I have to do?"

This guy doesn't give up so easily, I thought. "To begin with, show up at our training session tomorrow."

He did turn up, and immediately surprised everyone, despite his frail looks, with his splendid physical fitness. Several more days went by and we became convinced that Ledenev's character was equally dependable. And when Dmitri decided to test the newcomer with a troublesome problem we had been having with some of our equipment, Vladimir demonstrated real ingenuity. It was clear he was admirably suited to be the expedition's quartermaster.

He had spent his childhood in a small village some hundred kilometers from Moscow. Upon finishing school, he knew exactly what he wanted to do. Further his education, of course! Without any special effort he passed his entrance examinations to the Food Institute, majoring in automation and comprehensive mechanization of chemico-technological processes. He studied conscientiously and with the diligence of a village boy; in his leisure time, like the majority of students who are not well-off, he earned pocket money by working as a watchman, a stoker, a stevedore, and a train conductor. Besides extra money, these jobs gave him confidence in himself—a quality Ledenev displays.

In his sophomore year, he briefly took up skydiving. Though he delighted in soaring through the air, the club he belonged to fell apart when one of their jumps almost cost their coach his life; his parachute had opened just in time, practically at ground level, and the man rather understandably changed his profession.

He then switched to hiking. With a rucksack on his

148

back, he hiked through the Sayan Mountains and the area beyond Lake Baikal, through the Carpathian Alps and the Kola Peninsula. On one of his hikes he met a girl—not the talkative type, but as proud and clever and strong as Ledenev himself. Vladimir and Olga are perhaps the ideal married couple—or at least that is how they were once presented on a TV program for newlyweds.

Ledenev became a full-fledged member of our group in 1972, after the passage across Long Strait. During that expedition he was always the first to get up after a break (someone has to be the first to get to his feet, and it should never be forgotten how difficult that can be); he was always the first to volunteer to scout on up ahead when the group ran into a bad range of hummocks (when the rest of the team welcomed the excuse to rest); and he always responded to others' misfortunes.

Khmelevsky calls him "a one hundred percent regular guy": "For example, say the encircling disk comes off my ski pole but I keep on going, because what the heck. But if Vladimir saw it, without saying a word he would retrieve it and later repair it. And not just because he is responsible for the equipment, but because that is his nature—to fix things."

Amid the chaos of hummocks and open water I personally was amazed by his undying optimism. The ice cracked and piled up right under our feet—"Isn't that terrific!" Ledenev shouted. "That's what I call power!" The frost and wind whipped our faces mercilessly—"Isn't that great?" he exclaimed enthusiastically. "You won't find that in Moscow!"

And you should see him at training sessions! Particularly a football game. Fortunate is the team that has Ledenev. His style is a nonstop fight for the ball; he is everywhere on the field—passing, attacking, falling, helping the backs check an attack—and then he is off on a breakaway. No matter what the score, Ledenev keeps on fighting to the last second. Forward, and only forward! To him it does not matter who scores the goal—what is important is that the team wins. Football lays bare the core of his character.

Currently he is a senior scientist at the Research Institute of Fermentation, working on a new technology for the production of vodka. He grew along with the expedition. Its achievements were also the result of his own victories, his maturity as a man.

"Living and working with a group of friends sort of gave me my second wind," says Ledenev on this subject. "From Dmitri I learned persistence, from Vladimir Rakhmanov kindness, from Yuri stamina. The polar expedition has become my flesh and blood."

Vasili poured the fuel out of the jerry can directly onto the snow. The spot was yellow.

"Gasoline leaves a bluish tone."

"No doubt about it," said Ledenev. "It's solar oil. What a day to spoil. . . ."

"Hey everyone," he called out, "come on over here. I've got an announcement to make."

When everyone had gathered around him, having dropped what they were doing, Vladimir, without mincing words, made the announcement.

"Instead of gasoline they delivered solar oil, and the primus stoves will not work on that."

Everyone was taken aback.

"What the hell! Have they gone crazy over there?!" Rakhmanov cursed loudly and became white as a sheet. He spat into the snow, turned on his heel, and marched into the cold tent.

The rest of the men just stood there speechless.

Finally, Dmitri broke the silence. "Is there radio contact with NP-24?" he asked.

"I'll try," Melnikov sighed.

He entered the tent, switched on the station, and called the drifting station. Ivanov answered immediately.

"Stand by on reception," Melnikov spoke in a severe tone. "Also call Fyodor. We have an urgent message."

He poked his head out of the tent and proclaimed: "I've made contact."

Dmitri was thinking of what he was going to say to Fyodor. It was clear that now was not the time for a dressing-down. First of all, the men at NP-24 would feel as bad about their blunder as the skiers did. Second, the air is open to all listeners and there was no need to let the whole world eavesdrop on subordinates being reprimanded (though Shparo caught himself wishing he could really give them hell). Third, the situation had to be rectified as expeditiously as possible.

"Fyodor, can you hear me?"

"Yes, Dmitri," Sklokin replied. "I'm all ears."

"Fyodor. . . ." said Dmitri. He became silent so as to think over his next phrase.

Sklokin, who had long ago become accustomed to the chief's mannerisms, patiently waited.

". . . Say, Fyodor, has the IL-14 left for the mainland or is it still there?"

"It took off just a short while ago," Sklokin replied. "Why do you ask?"

"Why?!" Dmitri exploded. "I'll tell you why. Because instead of gasoline you dropped solar oil to us. Solar oil! Now do you understand why?"

Dmitri immediately checked himself and, feeling sorry for his outburst, continued in a calmer tone.

"We'll try to contact the airstrip at Chersky. You try to do the same on your service channel. You must find out whether there will be a plane during the next twenty-four hours from Chersky to NP-24. If there is one, the plane should detour our way and airdrop some gasoline. If there isn't one scheduled, they should send one any-

way. And don't forget: we haven't a single drop of gasoline in camp."

The fierce wind tore at the walls of the tent. Only
now did the skiers feel the sting of the cold and the wind-
driven snow. Five of them indecisively marked time at the
tent's entrance, while inside the stern voice of their chief
could be heard trying to straighten the matter out.

The first to come to his senses was Ledenev. Without
a word he got down to business: out of the casing of one
of the primus stoves he engineered a kind of fireplace,
then filled it with solar oil and set a match to it. Immediately a column of black smoke curled skyward. The snow
all around them blackened also, but now at least he could
try to cook supper. From the soot, the oatmeal and the
tea took on a blackish tone, but everyone ate and drank
without complaint. It was not long before their faces too
became black with soot; sitting there together, they looked
like a convention of sweeps.

Meanwhile, neither Shparo nor Melnikov budged
from the radio. Finally they managed to make contact with
a ham radio operator in Chersky named Mikhail Filippov.
It was not easy, considering Chersky was more than a
thousand kilometers away. From his apartment Filippov
phoned the airstrip and learned the flight schedule for
tomorrow. A flight was planned to NP-24. Through Filippov Dmitri passed on a message to the pilots, asking them
to fly out to the ski team and drop some gasoline. The
pilots immediately confirmed they would do this.

That evening Shparo made an interesting entry in his
diary: "Yuri and Vladimir pinpointed our position using
the stars. A bonfire of solar oil was burning near the theodolite. A candle was burning in the tent. Stars were twin-
kling in the sky. White evil ice surrounds us on all sides.
We were consoled by our radio contact. We do not feel
alone."

The next day the IL-14 appeared once again, and from

the sky a parachute carried down a drum of pure aviation gasoline.

White Stripes Followed by Black

They spent the first two days of April in the tent, virtually in a state of bliss. They could eat their fill, sleep as long as they wanted, dry their belongings, and take a rest from rucksacks that at times had seemed filled with lead. Almost continuously, two primus stoves burned in the tent, giving off a kind of warmth that had practically been forgotten. Without the stoves, the temperature inside the tent was only two or three degrees warmer than outside.

However, the reader should not think that the tent in any way resembled a normal human dwelling. No, it was a decidedly Spartan affair, designed for minimal weight, maximal ease in setting up, and dependability. Most ordinary tents sleeping six to eight persons weigh ten or twelve kilos. This one weighed 4.2. It provided fifteen square meters of floorspace, and its "ceiling" was 1.6 meters from the ground. The idea for its design was borrowed from the peoples of the North—the Chukchi and the Eskimos, who built their dwellings in the form of a conical tepee. This is a structure with very slight sail action, and the wind, no matter how powerful, only presses the tent closer to the ground.

To pitch the tent the skiers find a suitable stretch of ice (preferably old pack ice, without crevices) and throw off their rucksacks. Then, with a knife and a length of string, a circle is drawn on the snow (which as a rule is hard and packed), the knife making a shallow furrow. Then the butts of the skis are set in this furrow, and their tips locked together at the top with a titanium frame. Over this skeleton is thrown an orange kapron cover that forms the ceiling and walls. The bottom of this covering is inserted into the furrow all around and wedged tightly with blocks of snow. A special blue sleeve—the entrance—is then attached, and with a sewn-in cord can be drawn tight. The kapron covering allows the tent to breathe.

For considerations of weight and safety, the tent has no floor. In case of emergency (a sudden cracking of ice, a bear attack), it is much easier to escape from such a tent. Instead of a floor a sheet of polyethylene film is spread directly on the snow, on top of which everyone places his own foam mattress. All that is left to do then is to crawl into your sleeping bag, nuzzle closer to your comrades—the closer together, the warmer it is—and drift off. Two men can pitch the tent in ten to fifteen minutes.

There is not a lot of space in the tent, no extra elbow room, but seven men, sitting or lying under the kapron ceiling, do not feel overcrowded. At their feet, near the entrance, is an open area where the man on KP can perform his duties. His "batterie de cuisine" consists of two gasoline primus stoves, two pots, and metal utensils (seven cups, seven spoons, seven bowls).

After the second airdrop Vasili proposed that the parachutes be draped over the kapron covering for added warmth; when eventually the temperature one meter from the floor rose to plus five, Vadim suddenly said, "Why don't we take baths in here?"

Baths? The proposal was so unexpected that at first no one could say anything. On previous expeditions the question was not even brought up; it was simply taken for granted that in such severe weather baths were impossible. But since the present expedition was to last much longer than the usual three or four weeks, it had been arranged that the plane would drop them personal hygiene kits developed as part of the Soviet space program—moist napkins and towels made of antimicrobe cloth, dry towels. . . . It was assumed that during their longer rest stops the men would want to wipe their faces and hands with these towels.

But an actual bath? In the tent? On the snow?

"Well, why not?" exclaimed Dmitri. "It's not a bad idea. Let's give it a try."

Two large pots were already boiling on the primus stoves. Dmitri undressed at once, and Vadim began flogging him with towels dipped in the steaming water.

"Say, that's great! Better than a real bath," Dmitri grunted. Then washing his hair, drying it with a towel, and putting on fresh underwear, he slipped into his sleeping bag, his face literally glowing with pleasure. "Vadim," he purred, "you're a real genius."

Khmelevsky and Rakhmanov, who had been puttering around outside with the theodolite, were attracted by the joyful noise inside and peeked into the tent. Yuri was somewhat taken aback when he saw Ledenev standing about without a stitch on being flogged by Vadim.

"Bath time!" shouted Shparo. "You remember baths, don't you?"

"Oh, yes," Yuri came back quickly. "Quite normal —bath time at the old North Pole. Who's next in line? I don't want to miss my turn."

Vadim was the last to have his bath. There was no need to economize with the water—there was plenty of snow around. The primus stoves burned continuously, for there was also plenty of gasoline. When the bathing was over, they lounged about in their sleeping bags, sipping hot tea and reading letters and fresh newspapers from home. They also got around to discussing their plans for the next two weeks.

Khmelevsky had finished his astronavigational calculations and could joyfully report that the southerly drift seemed to have given way to the long-awaited northward one. In the past day, the ice they were on had taken them two kilometers closer to the Pole.

"Why don't we just let the drift do all the work?" Vadim suggested, almost half-seriously. "We could loll about like this in the tent, and wait for the Pole to come to us."

"So far," Rakhmanov laughed, "our chances are greater of floating back to Henrietta."

Davydov was happy his idea of taking baths had brought so much pleasure to his friends. Until then there had been no opportunity for him to display his medical acumen. Everyone was pretty healthy, not counting the frostbite of course, which by now everyone simply ignored. (His own toes had become so frostbitten that the skin was affected with dry gangrene, but he waved it off, saying "It's nothing.")

Vadim's credo as a doctor puts an emphasis on prevention. So as not to treat a person: that is how the physician should conduct himself.

"In Moscow I deal practically round the clock with people who are sick," Vadim once said to me. "I come to their aid, try to alleviate their suffering, and experience satisfaction in this. On a difficult trip, however, it's not possible to speak of sick people. But since there's a doctor along, people feel they must come up with at least some complaints. 'I've got a runny nose,' says one. 'That's normal,' I reply; 'you're in the Arctic.' 'I've got a bruised finger,' complains another. 'Think nothing of it,' I reply; 'it'll heal by itself.' " What Vadim is actually doing here is applying, in a very ingenious way, the method of psychotherapy. Though his medical bag contains more conventional remedies, he prefers to use them only when all else fails.

When I developed the film that was shot right before the ski team started out, the good doctor seemed to appear in every picture. Had I not known him better, I might have accused him of wanting to be the star of the show, but the real explanation is that Davydov is very photogenic, tall and extremely handsome. The camera lens seems naturally to seek him out.

Yuri calls him the typical sanguine type. And he is quite the family man as well. "For me my family, my two children, come first," Vadim explains. "Now Dmitri, don't be offended—my work in the hospital comes second. And the expedition comes in third."

Of the seven members of the team, Vadim is the only one who can consider himself a professional polar explorer: upon graduation from the First Medical Institute in Moscow, he elected to work in the Far North, and was sent to the northernmost airstrip in the country—on Franz Josef Land. He arrived there while the polar night ruled supreme, the sun never rising above the horizon. This is a time when the Arctic is especially harsh. One must have nerves of steel to live and work in darkness and in bitter cold, amid howling snowstorms and the mysterious Northern lights. The winter and the long polar night test a newcomer and his character to the limit.

But much to the surprise of all those around him, Davydov did not seem to notice these hardships. He worked with enthusiasm, and whenever he had spare time and the light of the moon was bright enough, he would sling his carbine over his shoulder and go for a hike. The North won his heart with its severe and reserved grandeur, its endless white expanses. Not once did he ever regret his decision—the work at that faraway airstrip proved a worthy introduction to what would follow.

On May 1, 1965, Davydov first laid eyes on the North Pole. On that day he volunteered to go out with some hydrologists on an ice recon patrol. The aircraft took off from Franz Josef Land and headed northward: they were approaching the very top of the planet.

"What does the Pole look like?" Vadim asked, pressing his face to the porthole. "I hope I don't miss it."

"Don't worry," the hydrologists assured him. "You'll see a circular icefloe, and from its center will be three hundred and sixty crevices radiating out in all directions—and right where they meet, that'll be the North Pole."

Vadim nodded his head and again began looking at the ice passing under the wings of the plane. Only when he heard a loud guffaw did he realize that they had been pulling his leg.

A year later, while working as physician to a big expedition, he made a landing at the Pole with a number of other scientists. Standing amid blue hummocks, and struck with the solemnity of the moment, he suddenly thought of how fine it would be to reach the Pole on foot, to conquer these endless expanses, the hummocks, the cold, and one's own fear. The time will come, he thought, when someone will do just that.

Upon his return to Moscow, he read about Shparo's group in *Komsomolskaya Pravda*. That day he said to his wife: "In three years you will see them getting ready to conquer the Pole."

Finally, in 1974, he found Dmitri's home telephone number through Moscow information and rang him up: "Does the expedition need a doctor?"

WHITE STRIPES FOLLOWED BY BLACK

It was quite a coincidence. Vadim had called just when Dmitri happened to be looking for precisely that: a medic for the expedition. They met, and from that day on Davydov was a full-fledged member of the team.

The next morning Davydov again caught everyone's attention. He announced he was going to start the medical part of the expedition's scientific program. First he examined their mouths and, at the request of the specialists at the Stomatology Institute, swabbed their gums and lips with iodine. Then he handed out tests containing scores of questions. In the opinion of scholars such testing would measure the psychological stability of each member of the team and the overall psychological climate in the group. Repeated testing would reveal the interrelational dynamics among members of the expedition.

With some good-natured grumbling the men armed themselves with pencils and began filling out the questionnaires. The first test, compiled by H. J. Eysenck, the British psychologist, consisted of fifty-seven questions aimed at determining a person's sociability and the stability of his physical state. "Do you like to joke and tell funny stories to your friends?" "Do your nerves let you down?" "Do you like being among people?" And so on and on.

The interest of psychologists in an expedition such as ours is easily explained. A group of people who are very nearly autonomous, having almost no contact with the outside world, is a convenient subject for investigations into group dynamics. How, and on the basis of what principles, should one choose small groups of people who must work together in conditions of prolonged isolation? How should duties be distributed among the members of the group? How should one chose the leader? What means can be used for maintaining an optimal psychological climate in the group?

Mikhail Novikov, whom we have already met, is a leading Soviet expert in psychology. He once tried to explain to me the meaning of "psychological compatibility."

"The appearance of this concept as a serious research problem is directly related to the emergence of rocket engineering and the quite real prospect of prolonged space flights involving not one, but several cosmonauts. Researchers began wondering: what would be the relationship among people who for a long period are confined to a small, closed cabin, without any opportunity to be by themselves, or to indulge their weaknesses? This is no idle question: the success of an entire space flight depends to a great extent on the psychological climate.

"Specialists differentiate two levels of compatibility: social and psychophysiological. The social level presumes a common understanding and acceptance of the objectives and assignments of the group. All members of the group must share a similar motivation, an identical worldview (or at least worldviews not directly contradictory), and a desire to cooperate. The psychophysiological level presumes a general similarity and pattern of emotional reactions, and an equal degree of physical fitness.

"The difficulties of studying these problems are aggravated by the fact that the development of personality in conditions of prolonged isolation cannot always be predicted. But even at present psychologists can offer very useful recommendations in cases in which a small group is being selected for an important assignment."

During those days the health of the skiers was a matter of concern for Moscow. And a definite role in this was played by Dmitri's dispatches to *Komsomolskaya Pravda*. They told a story of freezing temperatures, frostbite, that head-on drift. . . . In some quarters it all seemed far too dangerous. What if something happens? I wasted my breath trying to convince these Nervous Nellies that the cold and the wind are just as normal in the Arctic as heat is in the Sahara, and that the members of the group are inured to such hardships, that they feel quite normal.

"Normal?" I was asked. "If we had known ahead of time about the terrific cold, the hummocks, this drift. Perhaps we should drop them fur clothing?"

"You won't ski very far in furs."

"Then what kind of medicine do they need?"

"They need only one kind of medicine: progress toward the Pole."

"You're an optimist." They looked at me scornfully.

"I see no reason for pessimism," I snapped. The ability to be diplomatic, as always, had failed me.

And my hotheadedness was uncalled for: these people were in fact guided by good intentions—to somehow help the skiers, to make it easier for them. Their alarm was in excess, their advice naive, but so what?

A day the newspaper carried the latest dispatch from the Arctic, I received a telephone call from a very meticulous reader.

"Are there any errors in the article about the polar expedition?" he inquired.

"No errors," I assured him.

"And no exaggerations?"

"None whatsoever."

"All right," gloated the reader, as if he had caught me redhanded. "We'll see. Your article here says the rucksack of each member of the expedition weighs practically fifty kilos. Is that right?"

"Absolutely."

"And the article goes on to say that with such loads they spend the whole day clambering up icy hummocks?"

"Quite correct."

"Come on now!" the reader exclaimed indignantly. "With a fifty-kilo rucksack you won't go far even on the flat, to say nothing of those whatchamacallits . . . hummocks. No, there is something wrong here."

So I had to prove to this skeptic that everything was exactly as described in the article. I don't know whether I managed to convince him or not, but in any case, at the end of our telephone conversation he remarked with some amazement: "These skiers of yours must be like Hercules."

Actually, my friends have very little in common with Hercules. However, it is a fact that they are in superb physical shape. Eight years of regular training, a stringent, truly Spartan mode of life, and a series of arduous treks in the higher latitudes have left their mark. Not a single man in the group smokes, and they are very moderate when it comes to anything stronger than lemonade. There are, naturally, no prohibitions. Yet the very spirit of the expedition, the nature of their encounters excludes anything that might hinder their work.

Three times a week they hold their training sessions, which are conducted along lines endorsed by specialists in physical training. On Tuesdays and Fridays they train in the gym and the swimming pool, and on Sundays they go outdoors. In the autumn they take long cross-country hikes, and in the winter twenty kilometer ski trips with heavy rucksacks.

I no longer join them on their treks over the ice, but I am fond of participating in their training sessions, especially football games, when we traditionally split up into old timers and greenhorns.

Or take the sessions in the weightlifting room. You take an iron barbell disk weighing twenty kilos into your hands, or on your back, or on your chest, and the drills begin. Sklokin, the trainer of the expedition, knows dozens of exercises that can be done using the disk. I conscientiously lug mine around, but watch all the others out of the corner of my eye. The picture is indeed striking: ten well-built men keep hoisting the disk until they are almost totally fatigued. As usual, Dmitri shows his character:

salty sweat pours down his face, his t-shirt is soaked, but even so he keeps up his drills longer than all the rest. I noticed long ago that they are all especially zealous when it comes to weightlifting. They realize that in order to carry a fifty-kilo pack on your back for days on end, you have to be strong. You must be very strong.

Then comes tumbling. Watching from the sidelines one might think these men were just having a good time on the mats. But they are not playing. Tumbling helps you learn to fall correctly, without bruising yourself. And to be sure, there is plenty of falling to be done out on the ice.

The men never miss a chance to participate in marathons. Once they even participated in a hundred-kilometer race, and some twelve hours later crossed the finish line. Only one of them dropped out before the finish.

In Moscow, as usual, there were plenty of things to attend to. On March 31 the Pole-79 International Ham Radio Competitions were to begin. At a certain time on certain days Melnikov would go on the air, and the hams of the world were to make contact with the group. For each contact they were awarded a certain number of points, and the one with the highest score would be proclaimed the winner.

The objective of this competition was not simply to generate publicity. Radio contact with the ski team and the base camp—as I have already mentioned, such contact was in effect round-the-clock, with hundreds of volunteers involved all over the world—helped guarantee the safety of the expedition. We hoped that at any time of the day or night there would be someone out there who could contact the group.

At the beginning of the contest I arrived at the Central Radio Club, which had the intricate job of coordinating this mammoth undertaking. When I put on a pair of earphones, the airwaves were a veritable Babel. As a group, ham radio operators are a disciplined lot, but that morning they had cast off their usual restraint. Each was out to be the first to make contact with the ski team.

The chief of the radio station tried to bring a little order to this confusion. Pulling the microphone to him, he placed a sheet of clean paper on his desk, picked up a pencil, and said in a very strict voice to the entire world: "Let's queue up."

In a matter of minutes his list included the call letters of more than fifty radio stations—the Soviet Union, Bulgaria, Mongolia, Poland, Austria, Canada, the U.S.A., Japan.

"Czechoslovakia is also awaiting its turn," came an excited voice with a slight foreign accent.

At that moment five thousand kilometers away, at their ice camp in the Arctic Ocean, Shishkarev checked the connections of the antenna, the mast of which was made of ski poles. Meanwhile Melnikov made himself more comfortable in his sleeping bag, and tuned his radio (weighing just a bit more than two kilos and about the size of a carton of cigarets), and once again slowly repeated their new call letters—U-Zero-K. K for Komsomol. The expedition had been given these letters especially for the competition.

Labutin, many times shortwave champion of the USSR, took upon himself the role of controller for the competition. The list of ham operators on the "live line" was dictated to him from Moscow, and he accorded the privilege of opening the competition to *Komsomolskaya Pravda*, i.e., yours truly.

"Hello, Anatoli," I said in an excited voice, hardly able to imagine that five thousand kilometers away, inside a thin kapron tent, Melnikov would hear my voice.

"Hello there," came the cheerful voice of Anatoli. "How do you read me?"

166

"Loud and clear!" I realized that now was not the time to fill the air with a long conversation, and after general greetings I inquired: "How are you all feeling? We're concerned over Dmitri Shparo's dispatch regarding the severe cold."

"Don't worry about it. There's no cause for concern. The cold isn't bothering us any more than it ever has."

"Well, then, once again we wish you smooth and solid ice."

No sooner had I uttered these words than the air was once again filled with multilingual speech. Everyone was calling U-Zero-K. Then the stern voice of Labutin cut it short: "All right, everyone, let's follow the list."

The competition had begun.

On my way home from the Central Radio Club I found myself thinking that unknown people were linked to each other not so much by short waves as the desire to be useful to each other.

"I don't know about you, but I like it when life is like a zebra: white stripes followed by black. Everything balanced—white and black, the sweet and the salty."

This from the mouth of Rakhmanov the morning of April 5. Shishkarev immediately entered a most resolute objection, firmly convinced that man himself makes his own life as he wants it—black *or* white.

"Then make it so the hummocks are smaller," Dmitri let fly. "Make life easier for yourself."

Shishkarev stared daggers at him. "For me," he said, "the route does not seem so difficult. And you mock me in vain. Rakhmanov is talking like a typical idealist."

"And you, Vasili, too often you overestimate your strength," Dmitri jabbed.

"Me? Never! And I can prove it to all of you. I'll bet that in a year's time I can learn higher mathematics at least as well as you, professor. You want to bet?"

167

Sparks were flying, and in order to avoid a quarrel, Khmelevsky tactfully changed the subject. He was half afraid Vasili might really get down and start studying mathematics, and that would mean he was a goner as far as the expedition was concerned.

Rakhmanov had offered the zebra simile as a way of describing his attitude toward the spot, or stripe, they now found themselves in. Having started up again after two days of serene rest, they immediately found themselves in trouble. All the way to the horizon the ice piled up in heaps, as if someone had ripped through it with a giant plow. The skiers had set out with a great surge of energy only to land in this mess . . . and to begin marking time.

On April 3 Vadim had fallen through the ice into the cold water. He was fifth in line, just behind Rakhmanov. The new ice did not hold, and quick as that he found himself up to his waist in water. He cried "Help!" just once, in a rather muffled voice, and before he could summon a better effort Rakhmanov had yanked him out of the water and onto firm ice.

All the next day the group managed only four or five kilometers' progress. And to compound their problems, the weather took a turn for the worse: white mist blotted out the sun, and with it the gradations of light and shadow, the delicate chiaroscuro that signaled a rough spot, a ledge, a boulder of ice, that told them where they might safely put their feet. As a result, the skiers stumbled and fell. Their rucksacks, restocked since the airdrop, once again weighed a full fifty kilos.

That evening it was Melnikov's turn to prepare supper, and Shishkarev had taken over at the radio. He fumbled about a bit setting up the equipment, and at nine o'clock (the time of their regular contact) had still not gone on the air. Anatoli was just then dishing out the meal, so Vasili decided to have his supper first. It was not until nine-twenty that he finally switched on the transmitter and called Kotelny. "Labutin, Labutin. Come in, Labutin." The silence on the air waves was more chilling than the weather outside. Vasili summoned NP-24. Again no answer. Quickly running outside to check the antenna, he once again switched on the transmitter, summoning in turn Kotelny, NP-24, Chersky, and, finally, anyone who might hear him. Nobody did. It seemed that except for them there was not a soul in the entire world. Not a single dot or dash of Morse code, not even a bit of static could be heard.

When he saw that Vasili was having trouble, Melnikov dropped his cooking and joined him at the radio. The two of them were able to determine that the equipment was in perfect order. Now the gaze of the other five became focused on them. Shparo was particularly nervous: daily contact with the base camps was extremely important to him.

"Well, are we going to make contact?" he asked again and again.

To this Vasili said nothing, while Anatoli, busy puttering around with the equipment, would offer a "we'll see" or an "anything can happen." Finally the rest of the men, all but Shparo, got tired of his fussing around and decided to hit the sack. Dmitri became more and more gloomy, but did not take his eye off the radio operators.

"The radio signals are not getting through," declared Melnikov. "We might as well stop trying; we're not going to get through."

"You're absolutely sure of that?"

"Let's check it out," said Anatoli. He fished around in his rucksack a bit and extracted the small Orbita transistor radio he used to pick up regular broadcast stations for time checks. "If the signals are not getting through, then in the Arctic that means all wave bands."

He switched on the transistor and spun the dial. Silence. Melnikov looked up at his comrades.

"That's the treachery of shortwaves," he said. "Magnetic storms simply put them under a padlock."

"But can't you do anything?" As usual, Dmitri was not about to give up.

Melnikov just shrugged his shoulders, while Shishkarev mumbled Labutin's call letters into the microphone. Vasili felt a bit guilty about going on the air late. Who knows, perhaps exactly at nine the magnetic storm had not yet cut them off.

For another hour and a half they sat up in the hope of making contact. Finally Dmitri sighed deeply and crawled into his sleeping bag. He was disappointed because he had not managed to send out a number of important dispatches, and because they had to do without tomorrow's weather forecast. But most of all he was upset because of the very fact they could not make contact. The expedition's radio communications system was his pride and joy; until today it had not once let them down.

All this time Labutin had been trying, in vain, to make contact with the ski team. Having concluded that the magnetic storm had blocked out all short-wave signals in the area, he switched on his medium-wave transmitter and, as had been prearranged for such circumstances, roused Sklokin at NP-24. Fyodor confirmed that the short waves were not getting through. The magnetic storm was so powerful that one could not pick up even the signals of the satellite working in the USW-band. Labutin had greater faith in the satellite transmitter than perhaps anyone—he had assembled it with his own hands.

The next day was no easier. The surface seemed absolutely hopeless for skiing, and was not much better for walking. The ice, three to four meters thick, was broken, crushed, contorted into jagged shapes as far as the eye could see. How could this have happened out here in the open ocean? Hummocking like this usually occurs near land. There it is easier to explain: the ice, pressing against solid land, breaks up and piles itself in heaps. Out here it is far more complicated.

The greater part of the day was devoted to ice reconnaissance: the men fanned out in pairs to left and right in an effort to find a more or less traversable route. But each time they returned with nothing favorable to report.

Eventually they were so fatigued they decided to stop for the night an hour early. Fortunately, they had no trouble establishing radio contact that evening.

This was also the day they first saw fresh polar bear tracks; the paw marks stretched out in a line from west to east. That gave them something to think about, for now they were at least four hundred kilometers from the closest island, and zoologists claim that polar bears usually keep close to land—the open water there makes it easier for them to hunt seals. So even among wild animals, it would seem, there are daring travelers, wanderers over the whole ocean. . . . The tracks were fresh and suggested that a large she-bear with two cubs had just passed by, perhaps to hide behind the next hummock. Vadim, who was custodian of the armory, unfastened the ten-shot carbine strapped to his rucksack and dropped a cartridge into the firing chamber.

Polar bears are rightfully called "the masters of the Arctic." Past experience with this beast—the largest quadruped found north of the Arctic Circle—has taught us always to be on guard and to keep a weapon handy, as these bears often turn up quite unexpectedly. By its nature the polar bear is not particularly aggressive, but its curiosity may sometimes lead it too far. An international convention prohibiting the hunting of polar bears has led to an increase in their number, until today, according to zoologists' estimates, there are more than twenty-five thousand of them in the world. Men wintering at polar stations do not venture even a step from their doors without a gun. Polar bears regularly steal the pelts of seals and fox that are hung up for drying; they break into sheds and larders; in short, they behave like bandits. Especially unceremonious are young bears, who have not yet learned to be afraid, and very large, experienced specimens. The latter will not give way even to a tractor; to this day they consider themselves sole rulers of the Arctic.

I remember our first encounter with a polar bear. We were on Severnaya Zemlya and had stopped for the night. Yuri, as always, busied himself pitching the tent, while Dmitri prepared to cook supper right out in the open. He dug a small hole in the snow for the primus stove, while I picked up the saw and started cutting out blocks of packed snow. For supper we were to have dehydrated sausage. This highly nourishing product, an almost weightless powder that comes sealed in tinfoil, is placed in a bowl, hot water is poured over it, and in a split second you have an appetizing chunk of meat before you.

With our bowls in hand we were already stepping up to the table made of snow blocks when Boris Lyubimov—he was with us on that expedition—stammered out, "Look—a bear!"

There was a moment of slight confusion. As none of us had any experience with polar bears, we of course didn't know what to do.

Luckily the bear gave us time to collect our thoughts. He moved toward our camp without haste, but with great dignity. Occasionally he would stop, rear up on his hind legs like a circus bear, and sniff at the air, his nose like an antenna. Then he would continue on his way—directly toward us.

"He's probably half blind," I said. "As soon as he spots us, he'll hightail it. Too bad! It would be good to get a closer look at him. Maybe get photographed with him as a souvenir of our meeting."

"You'd better load the carbine," Dmitri advised. "The flare gun too."

172

Our sausage was getting colder by the minute. Meanwhile the bear was still headed our way. The smell of food had apparently so captivated him that he was completely oblivious to danger. Or perhaps he did not even know the meaning of danger, since every living thing feared him; possibly this was the first time he had ever seen human beings. In any case, the bear came so close to us that you could have thrown a mitten at him. We had long since put away our cameras and taken up arms. The bear picked up a rucksack in his paw and pulled it to himself as easily as if it were a feather. Yuri, whose rucksack it was, became quite offended. "Scat!" he shouted indignantly; then he gave a whistle and heaved a ski pole at the beast. When the bear did not react even to this blow, all of us felt offended.

"Shoot!" Yuri cried out.

Flares went flying in the direction of our uninvited guest. One, two, three. The bear growled ferociously, bared his teeth, then slowly turned and went romping gaily off to where the flares were shooting sparks into the snow. We all sighed with relief and sat down to finish our cold sausage.

The bear sniffed the smouldering flares, shook his head with displeasure, sending ripples along the powerful muscles of his body, and then headed once again in our direction. The situation was becoming serious.

Yuri began quoting from the regulations governing the safety of those working in the Arctic: "In view of the fact that the polar bear is now under the protection of the law, they may be killed only in self-defense. . . ."

The bear strode aggressively toward us.

". . . first of all a flare should be shot at the bear; usually in this case the bear is frightened and runs away."

"This bear, it seems, has not read the regulations," Dmitri said dryly.

"Author, author!" Boris muttered, flare pistol at the ready.

When there were about ten steps between us and the bear, carbine and flare pistol thundered simultaneously. The bullets ricocheted off the ice with an ear-splitting whine and went flying into the Arctic expanse. For a second we were almost deafened.

The bear jumped sharply back, but then, in no hurry whatsoever, trotted back to where he had come from. About two hundred meters away he stopped, sat on his haunches, and stared in our direction as if nothing had happened. Long past our usual bedtime, the master of the Arctic sat there, by all indications very hungry, and, in utter disregard of regulations, refused to be afraid of us. The situation was both quite funny and a little bit scary.

All our attempts to chase the bear away were futile. In the end we shrugged our shoulders: que sera sera. We drank our fill of salty tea (in this spot the snow was not deep and sea water had seeped through it) and left one man on guard duty. The rest of us, our weapons beside us, fell fast asleep.

As we emerged from our tent the next morning, the sort of cloudy mist that heralds a snowstorm had settled in. But through it we could see the handsome beast still sitting in the very same spot as yesterday, yellowish fur against the white snow, standing guard over all his domain.

Another dangerous animal for travelers in the Arctic is the walrus. An encounter with this beast while crossing open water by boat holds nothing good in store. In 1976, on the way from Wrangel Island to NP-23, three members of the expedition were almost drowned by a walrus. Dmitri told me about it.

"Very early in the journey, while we were still not far from the island, the ice field began cracking in all directions. The cracks grew and spread out right before our eyes, becoming broad streams of dark, steaming water. As quickly as we could, we inflated a large rubber liferaft.

174

"The first to cross were Rakhmanov, Davydov, and Khmelevsky. But before they could reach the other side, two walruses surfaced near them. Then, just as they thought they had made it, one of the walruses butted the heavily laden raft with its head, knocking it sideways as if it were a toy. The walrus leaped high into the air, like a water polo player, and came down with a huge splash, spraying the men in the boat with ice-cold water.

" 'I'm going to shoot,' Vadim shouted.

" 'He's simply playing,' I replied in a doubtful tone.

" 'This isn't the time for games. He'll puncture the raft,' Yuri said in a high-pitched voice.

"Nevertheless I hesitated, and so far did not allow any shooting: a wounded animal can be very dangerous. Finally the raft reached solid ice, but the walrus kept swimming around the icefloe, preventing a second crossing. There was no time to waste.

" 'Shoot!' I ordered.

"Davydov fired. The walrus disappeared under the water and surfaced far away from us. He seemed gravely wounded. The second walrus had disappeared entirely, and we were able to complete the crossing with no further trouble."

This is why Vadim always carried a ten-shot carbine and fifty cartridges. Perhaps he would not have to fire a single shot, but even so. . . .

The events of the days that followed are reported in the entries of Yuri Khmelevsky's diary.

"*April 7.* Yesterday Dmitri started lagging behind—it was obvious that every step was torture for him. Very quietly, so that no one else would hear, he complained to me that he felt weak and nauseated. Is this the result of fatigue? I myself experienced the very same symptoms today: the rucksack seemed to weigh a ton, my legs were wobbly, and I vomited. By evening the same thing had happened to Vasili.

175

"Davydov's diagnosis: food poisoning. Then the debate began: what had caused it? Rakhmanov said the parachute fabric was to blame. He claimed it was saturated in some harmful chemical substance, and the salt pork had been wrapped in it. Davydov was convinced that the salt pork itself had spoiled. I thought we had poisoned ourselves with the dehydrated cottage cheese. As usual, the debate continued for a long time. In his authority as a physician, Vadim imposed a veto on consumption of salt pork. For Vasili, Dmitri, and myself he prescribed a stringent diet and antibiotics.

"*April 8.* Somehow, Labutin found out that four days ago Vasili had been late in making radio contact. In view of this Leonid transmitted the following directive: 'Because of the whims of radio wave promulgation I ask you to comply with the set timetables. Otherwise this may give rise to a false alarm.' Judging by the officious tone, Labutin was really sore.

"*April 13.* Today, I took my second dip. This is how it happened. We had to cross a patch of water covered over with a thin coat of fresh ice. We decided to cross it on skis, taking all possible precautions. The main safety measure in this case involved the big rubber liferaft we carried. We inflated it, and the first two men, holding on to it on both sides, set out across the ice. Ledenev was to starboard; I was portside. We had covered a scant ten meters when suddenly a huge crack appeared directly under the raft, between Ledenev and myself. Vladimir instinctively leaped to the right, away from the crack. What was I to do? Continue on my way, abandoning the raft, or hold on to it and take a swim? These options flashed through my mind simultaneously, and I chose the second. Almost immediately I was up to my neck in water. But with my right hand I had a firm hold on the raft, into which Ledenev had somehow managed to jump. From there he was able to haul me out of the water.

"Of course I should have jumped into the raft the minute I saw the crack, but I thought to myself: 'Wouldn't I look stupid doing that?'

"It is interesting that this time my dip in the ocean did not upset me at all. As I was going down I even searched for the bottom with my feet: I simply couldn't believe that at this spot the ocean was over two thousand meters deep. The high banks of ice on either side of the freshly frozen patch of water created the impression of a shallow stream.

"Now I was absolutely convinced that a man who falls through the ice in the Arctic risks practically nothing. The main thing is not to panic, not to lose your head. Your comrades will always help you out of the water; then all you have to do is change your clothing and you can keep on moving.

"*April 14.* The time for the second airdrop is fast approaching, and much of our talk centers around the question of whether the aircraft can make a landing on the ice. Allegedly, such a landing has been requested by the doctors, who want to examine the group in mid-journey, as well as by cameramen shooting a film about the expedition and certain staff members from headquarters. An AN-2 aircraft can easily reach us if it flies out from NP-24, which at the moment is only a hundred and fifty kilometers to our west. Dmitri continues to have long conversations with Sklokin and Snegirev. Shparo, Ledenev, and I are against the landing, whether by plane or by helicopter. In a roundabout way Davydov formulates his opinion: 'If a plane lands, we'll be able to change our wet sleeping bags for dry ones.' Rakhmanov adds: 'We'll be able to pass on to the mainland all our deadweight—film, diaries, our scientific observations. The rest of the team are undecided. Ledenev is categorical on the issue: 'Even if headquarters makes the decision to land, we must set up our camp on an icefield that will make it impossible.'

177

"An extraordinary thing happened in the tent this evening: the carbine went off. The bullet passed through Vadim's rucksack and went into the ice. Vadim cannot understand how it could have happened. Someone accidentally knocked over the carbine while it was standing in the corner, but he swears the safety catch was on. The debate over whether to receive an aircraft or not is still raging."

My own entries from these days abound with the same questions: should the plane make a landing on the ice, or should all the necessary cargo be airdropped like the first time?

I was tormented by contradictions. On the one hand, I wanted to meet my comrades, to see for myself that they were alive and healthy, and, what is most important, to exchange ideas on a whole number of questions (not everything can be discussed by radio). I could also understand the doctors, the cameramen, and my journalist colleagues wanting to meet up with the skiers. I saw the advantages of live contact, and also the merits of what Davydov and Rakhmanov had to say. But all the same, I was kept from making a firm decision in favor of such a meeting by the very thing that made Dmitri reject the help of a helicopter during the start from Henrietta. Perhaps I was being finicky, too concerned over the reputation of the expedition, but all of us—Shparo, Khmelevsky, Ledenev, and myself—shared the same feeling. We had put too many years and too much work into this struggle for the Pole, to be indifferent now toward what might be said about the expedition once it was completed. One careless decision now and we might be sorry about it the rest of our lives.

Fortunately, many people at headquarters shared our opinion, and ended up by leaving the decision to Shparo.

On April 13 I flew to Chersky from Moscow. As soon as I had taken up accommodations in the hotel for flyers,

I sat down at the radio station. Following is a transcript of the conversation.

Kotelny Island (Labutin): Coordinates of the ski group on April 12—81°01' north latitude, 157° east longitude. Day temperature, minus thirty-five; night, minus forty. All members of the ski team feel fine. Good mood. On April 12 the group stopped for the night before a patch of open water approximately one kilometer wide. This morning, April 13, after ice reconnaissance patrol, the crossing is to be made. In view of this, the base radio stations will be operating in the emergency mode, i.e., receiving all the while.

Chersky (Snegirev): Got your report. Now let's discuss working matters.

Kotelny. As concerns communications, question No. 1 is redeployment of the main radio station from Kotelny to NP-24. The group is moving farther north and radio contact is bound to become more difficult. I believe we should therefore move our more powerful equipment closer to the Pole.

Chersky. I was expecting something like that. I promise I'll think it over and notify you as soon as possible. I hope you understand that it is not all that simple.

Kotelny. Of course I understand. The operation requires detailed planning. It probably has to be brought up at a meeting back at headquarters. The next problem concerns the airdrop. Do you know when and how it is to be carried out?

Chersky. According to the schedule, on April 16. From NP-24 we will be flying out on two planes. An IL-14 will drop the containers, while cameramen and journalists can observe the operation from an AN-2.

Kotelny. Roger. But we have some additional thoughts here from Fyodor and Dmitri regarding the possible landing of a plane. Have you heard these suggestions?

Chersky. No, I haven't. I know only that Dmitri is categorically opposed to landing any aircraft at their camp.

179

Kotelny. Well, now there is an idea of making a landing without actually meeting up with the group. The AN-2 would land in the vicinity of the camp—say, two kilometers ahead of their northward route—and you could there unload the cargo for the skiers. They in turn would leave everything that is to be taken back to the mainland.

Chersky. Perhaps we could offer Dmitri this variant: the plane would make a landing at some distance from the camp, and Shparo and I would meet halfway between the camp and the plane—on neutral territory, so to speak.

Kotelny. We've discussed precisely that many times over. At first Dmitri seemed to favor the idea, but Fyodor quite reasonably reminded him that this might give grounds for false rumors.

Chersky. Well . . . Fyodor is right, of course. This is something we cannot ignore.

Kotelny. Yes, it could quite possibly spoil the whole works. Nullify the whole project. What do people on the mainland think?

Chersky. There's a difference of opinion at headquarters. Like us, they understand the pros and cons. They like the concept of a "pure" experiment. I must contact Dmitri to discuss this.

Kotelny. According to schedule, the next contact, as always, will be 1330. Will you wait?

Chersky. By all means.

Group (Shparo): Hello, Vladimir. Once again I'm happy to welcome you in the Arctic. Shall we get down to brass tacks right away?

Chersky. Yes—hi there, Dmitri. Shoot.

Group. We want the drop to be carried out by the IL-14—without it making a landing. Do you understand?

Chersky. Roger—no landing. It's a pity we won't see each other, but I leave this question fully in your hands.

Group. Do you personally agree with my decision? What's your real opinion?

180

Chersky. That's a tough one. Frankly, I have no clear-cut opinion. I'd like to see all of you and discuss all our problems in person, but, on the other hand, I fully realize what talk might result if the aircraft made a landing. That is why I repeat, I leave this question fully in your hands.

On April 15 we flew from Chersky to NP-24, where the airdrop operation was to originate. The plane carried cameramen from the Central Film Studios for Popular Science and a leading Soviet journalist, Vasili Peskov, equally adept at writing and photography.

The Most Dangerous Enemy

By that time Sklokin's group at NP-24 had settled in quite comfortably. Their prefabricated wooden quarters were quite crowded but very cozy. In the corner farthest from the entrance stood the bunks, while by the door a solar oil stove burned constantly; it breathed out warmth, drying the clothes hanging above it, and one could always boil a kettle of water on it for tea. On a table near the window were the radio station and two recorders for taping conversations with the ski team. The walls were plastered with telegrams sent to the expedition from all corners of the globe.

Right next to their quarters they had pitched a large army field tent that served as a warehouse. When we landed, Fyodor was in the tent packing containers for the drop. After the recent mix-up with the solar oil, he was being especially careful.

That day at the station the temperature was minus forty. However, since the sun no longer hid below the horizon all day long, the cold did not seem all that bad. The hoarfrost sparkled like tinsel on a Christmas tree; the snow squeaked merrily underfoot. The cold prickled your face, but almost playfully it seemed. You could breathe deep and feel very free.

It was with a feeling of intense curiosity that my companions inspected the world's northernmost settlement. Drifting scientific stations like this one date from May 21, 1937. On that day four Soviet aircraft made a landing at the Pole to organize the first such station in history, NP-1.

Four men out of that party remained to live and work on the icefloe—Ivan Papanin, chief of the station; Ernst Krenkel, radio operator; Pyotor Shirshov, hydrologist; and Yevgeni Fyodorov, astronomer and magnetologist. Their 274-day drift is one of the most heroic chapters in the history of Arctic exploration. This was the first comprehensive study ever undertaken of the Arctic regions closest to the Pole. Hardly a day went by that Papanin's group did not make some sensational discovery or other, so meager was the store of knowledge at that time regarding ice drifts, underwater currents, ocean depths, weather conditions, and fauna in that area. Until that time the northern Arctic was indeed terra incognita.

At the beginning of 1938 the icefloe carrying NP-1, having traveled twenty-five hundred kilometers, was adrift in the Greenland Sea. On February 19, their mission completed, Papanin and his group closed their station and boarded the icebreakers *Murmansk* and *Taimyr*, which had come to pick them up.

For Soviet scientists it has become standard practice to study the Arctic Ocean from these drifting stations. Today, however, they are set up not at the Pole, but somewhere north of Wrangel Island; the camp then slowly traces an intricate line and moves toward the "top of the world." At times the station finds itself directly at the Pole. But more often it drifts past it into the Greenland Sea or, swerving to the right, comes full circle, returning to the initial starting area north of the Chukchi Peninsula. The station is abandoned if the icefloe is dragged westward and it becomes difficult for aircraft to reach it, or if the icefloe breaks up. In order to avoid the latter, scientists have in recent years begun locating the stations not on ice fields created at sea by the action of the cold, but on icebergs, hunks of glacial ice that have broken off and slid into the sea. There are not many of these in the ocean, and today all of them have been identified. They are regularly spotted and their positions noted by specially equipped aircraft or satellites.

NP-24 is located on an iceberg seventeen kilometers long and six wide; it weighs three billion tons and has an average thickness of thirty meters. The station was opened on May 31, 1973, and has a year-round population of nineteen people. When we arrived, it held three times that number, ourselves included, as spring is a time for seasonal expeditions.

Since the days of Papanin, much has changed in the life of polar explorers. Instead of tents they live in cozy prefabricated homes with electricity, heating, and up-to-date radio equipment. There is a great variety of scientific instruments and devices at the station, as well as tractors and snowmobiles. Aircraft from the mainland make regular flights, delivering fresh food, mail, new movies. Papanin's men could not even dream of such comforts. However, the two main hardships of life on the drifting stations have not changed much—the constant cold and the feeling of being cut off from civilization.

On April 15, at 2300 hours (Moscow time), Shparo came on the air. He reported the coordinates of the camp—81°38' north latitude, 156°40' east longitude. We agreed on a detailed exchange of information by radio after the drop. Shparo also agreed to answer questions from the journalists at that time.

Then last-minute preparations for the flight were made. The station's cook, Pasha Volkov, whom we have seen before, prepared a hot meal as a surprise treat for the skiers: beet soup, roast goose and potatoes, a salad, and, as the *pièce de résistance,* a cake baked for Vasili Shishkarev's thirtieth birthday. All this was packed neatly into a bag with a shock-absorbing lining and attached to a parachute.

On April 16 at 0115 (Moscow time), Peskov, two cameramen, and I took off on board the AN-2 and headed out for the ski team. Twenty minutes later the IL-14 with Sklokin and all the containers and parachutes lifted off from NP-24. At 0215 both aircraft arrived in the area of the coordinates Dmitri had given. Almost immediately the radio operator of our "Annie" pressed his finger to his lips as if to say "don't bother me; I hear the group." Melnikov's voice came over the USW-band. He said he could see us somewhat south of their camp, and then quickly gave both aircraft directions that brought them directly to the group. Everything went off quickly and smoothly.

The IL-14 got down to work. After several "targeting" passes it began dropping the cargo by parachute, while from the slower AN-2, circling a bit higher, photographers and cameramen shot the whole operation through the open hatch. The filming lasted about an hour. With its engine roaring the plane went into steep dives, and the ice would seem to be rising upward toward us. The biting wind lashed our faces. Yet all this paled to insignificance compared to the picture we saw below, a picture we wanted to capture not only on film, but forever in our hearts.

Down below us, on the wavy snow drifts covering

the old pack ice, stood a once orange, but now bleached, almost yellow tent. Next to the tent, a red flag fluttered from the antenna mast made of ski poles. A little farther away we could easily make out a cross made of green sleeping bags—a signal for the aircraft. But the most remarkable detail of that picture was the group of seven men in blue parkas. Against the background of the merciless Arctic, in the vicelike grip of the cold, the men did not seem so very helpless or pitiable. On the contrary, the entire picture we observed from the air was one of confidence, strength, and triumph.

We waved our hats at them and shouted words of encouragement—drowned out, of course, by the roar of the motor—while from below the men shot up flares to greet us. No doubt the skiers below us were excited too, but theirs was not the thrilling excitement we felt, but a more dignified excitement, a feeling of pride and confidence in oneself.

On the USW-band Dmitri summoned me for a talk.

"We've received all the cargo safe and sound," he said. "On behalf of all of us thank the pilots for a brilliant operation. The parachutes came down right at the entrance of our tent—incredible accuracy. What are the ice conditions around us?"

"You're on a huge field of pack ice. Some five kilometers northward along your projected route we spotted a recently frozen-over patch of water about two to four hundred meters wide. To both west and east it stretches out to the horizon, so don't try to go around it. While you rest here the ice there will probably become strong enough to hold you. An interesting situation has just developed to the south of your camp, approximately two kilometers from where you stand. When we first spotted you, a barely noticeable crack had just split the ice there. In the hour since then the crack has widened to the breadth of a large river, and there are some pretty big waves on it now."

"Thanks for the information. Everything clear. Till we speak again!"

Our "Annie" came around and soon we were homeward bound. The flight engineer, who had been worked up over the possibility that one of us might fall out of the open hatch, heaved an obvious sigh of relief as he secured it. Now was a time to catch our breath. Peskov was pleased with the filming; his eyes shone with excitement.

"You know, Vladimir, I'm a happy man. I have just seen some real men. I simply can't imagine that they have already covered five hundred kilometers over that ice." He looked through the porthole. "Not everyone can do that."

"One in a million, that's my opinion."

"You're right," agreed Peskov. "One in a million."

He was silent a moment, seemingly trying to fathom all he had seen. Finally he said, "When I saw the tent down below, the red flag, and the small figures of the men, tears came to my eyes."

At 0420 we were back at NP-24. We were all in dire need of sleep. For almost forty-eight hours we had been on our feet, and there were still plenty of things to attend to. On a special radio band I transmitted to Moscow an official dispatch detailing the successful completion of the airdrop, and this was followed by a report to headquarters we had just received from the ice camp, summing up the work of the expedition over the past month.

The report indicated that by the calculations of the expedition's navigator, Yuri Khmelevsky, the overall southward drift of the ice during the month was sixty kilometers. As yet there was practically no compensating northward drift. In thirty-one days, the report noted, the expedition had traveled 564 kilometers north, once the southerly drift was subtracted. The average progress of the ski group was therefore eighteen kilometers a day. Further, Shparo informed headquarters of the low tem-

188

peratures (sometime lower than minus forty-two). "However," he emphasized, "the cold is much more bearable than in March, since in the daytime the sun now heats the air and, the men have by now adapted themselves to the conditions around them." The report noted also that the hummocking had become considerably less serious now that they were out over great ocean depths. All members of the expedition were in excellent physical condition.

"All this," wrote Dmitri, "enables us to project an increase in the number of skiing hours to nine hours a day. This will add three kilometers a day to our northward progress. And should a northward drift appear, as we are certain it will, this will give us another two kilometers. If we can travel twenty-four kilometers daily, we can reach the North Pole in forty-two days."

At 0740 the ski group again came on the air. Audibility was perfect: not only could we make out various intonations of speech, but we could even hear them laughing and joking around in the tent. It was obvious they were in a good mood.

Shparo reaffirmed that the drop had been a perfect bull's-eye. He thanked Pasha for a delicious lunch, and Peskov for the seven twigs of budding willows he had inserted in one of the containers. Peskov had brought the willow branches with him from the countryside near Moscow, so that in the midst of the icy hummocks the skiers would be able to sense the live aroma of spring, the blossoming of a Russian forest.

For almost three hours the team participated in a radio press conference and replied to various questions concerning their day-to-day activities. Here is a partial transcript of that exchange.

"Dmitri, what so far has been the most unexpected thing to happen?"

"Unexpected? Give me a half a minute to think. I don't think anyone could have expected our skis to sink.

We thought that since they're made of wood they would float."

"Have there been any amusing or funny incidents?"

"Sure. One occurred just recently, during a crossing. Yuri Khmelevsky broke through the ice and his clothing was soaked, so we had to change him into something dry. Someone remembered the red kapron parka and matching trousers that were designed for the man on KP in case of a snowstorm: since the wet snow does not stick to Kapron, it makes it more convenient if you have to come out of the tent. So Khmelevsky was dressed all in red, and his old canvas suit, thoroughly soaked and salty, had to be discarded. He became quite a standout in that suit, a real beacon. You couldn't help noticing him. So all of a sudden some of the others, Vadim in particular, began saying they wouldn't mind having a good-looking suit like that themselves. But Ledenev, the quartermaster, is adamant: if you want a red parka, he says, you have to first take a swim."

"What do you feel you lack?"

"Vasili Shishkarev—the youngest and most energetic of us all—complains he doesn't get enough to eat. Vadim Davydov would like to receive more letters. Vladimir Ledenev, who is making movies, says that what he lacks is an encounter with a polar bear."

"In the opinion of the famous Norwegian explorer Roald Amundsen, man can become accustomed to almost anything—but not to the cold. What do you think?"

"I think that human beings, if they have to, can get used to it."

"How are things in terms of the group's psychological compatibility?"

"Perfect! The conditions for living here on the ice and the trek itself are very severe. There is absolutely not a single living creature around us. We know that in order to emerge from this ordeal in triumph, we must be a very close-knit group. If it were not for our friendship, it would be simply impossible to survive all this."

190

"How are ski conditions?"

"Different at different times of the day. When it is very cold and the sun then heats the snow a little, it becomes very slippery. Yet there are places where we run into granular snow, and there is no sliding at all. Fresh ice through which salt has surfaced is always very difficult, though fortunately the slush that results does not stick to our skis."

"What's your favorite dish on the trek?"

"First of all, we're proud of our diet—it's balanced, and we have complete faith in it. As for our favorite dish, I guess that would be condensed milk with sugar, generously laced with melted butter. It's high in calories, and was a truly reviving dish when we were all suffering from the severe cold. Now it is not that cold, and once again our favorite dish, as in past years, is dehydrated cottage cheese."

"Dmitri, is there anything you would like to pass on to our readers?"

"Let me think . . . I can't put it into a couple of words. I would like each reader of *Komsomolskaya Pravda* to share with us the great feeling of joy we experience every minute, every hour, every day. The joy of our struggle, and the realization that we are approaching our long-standing goal."

The third stage of the trek to the Pole was distinguished by unprecedented speed: in fourteen days the group covered four hundred kilometers. One by one, the 82nd, the 83rd, the 84th parallels were left behind.

The group kept stringently to the daily timetable—that was the most important guarantee of success. At 0430 the man on duty would rise to cook breakfast. At 0530 came general reveille and breakfast time. At 0730 the group began moving. At 1220 they stopped for lunch (they pitched their tent, the navigators measured the position of the sun, they ate and then had a half-hour nap after lunch). From 1500 to 2000 they made another five legs. At 2120 they knocked off for supper, processed the astro-navigational data, and made radio contact. At 2230 the skiers went to bed, although Dmitri's conversation with the base camps usually lasted until midnight.

I believe it was not by accident that Dmitri authorized Vasili to monitor the schedule and to check the time of all the operations. Shishkarev acted with the inexorability of a company sergeant major: if the schedule said there was to be ten minutes of rest after fifty minutes of skiing—that meant no one would get a second more. When the ten minutes were up, Vasili, without saying a word, would get up, put the rucksack on his back, and march forward. If you didn't follow suit, it meant you would have to make double time to catch up, or would have less time to rest at the next stop. The tent had to be dismantled and packed by 0700 each morning, and you could be sure it was. Vasili would yank the kapron coating from the frame. There could be someone half-naked inside; someone could be hastily packing his belongings, asking Vasili to wait just a moment; a snowstorm could be raging outside—no matter, Shishkarev was adamant. Without uttering a word he would fold the kapron and pack it into the rucksack. Because all seven of them had voted for such a stringent timetable, no one could be very offended at Vasili.

Only once did anyone fly off the handle and give their tormentor any trouble. One morning Melnikov had not managed to dismantle and pack his radio equipment—he was doing it when Vasili, in his usual taciturn manner, pulled the cover from the tent frame, leaving the half-dressed Melnikov without a roof over his head. Just then a sudden gust of wind sent snow all over the equipment. Anatoli raised his head slowly and stared daggers at Vasili. For several days thereafter they contrived not to notice each other. But this was a rare incident; in general, the psychological microclimate was favorable, good mood and good relationships prevailing.

The most difficult thing was getting up in the morning. To get out of a sleeping bag that had been warmed by your own body, and to find yourself the next moment in a thirty-degree frost is not an easy thing to do. Reveille was usually sounded by the man on duty. "In five minutes I'm going to start dishing it out," he would say, hinting that whoever did not rise immediately might go hungry.

Khmelevsky was a bit more courteous on duty. ("All right lads, is any one ready to have breakfast?"), while Ledenev was the exact opposite; filling each man's bowl, he would give each sleeping bag an unceremonious shove and hold out the bowl. Whether you wanted it or not, you had to get up and eat breakfast.

After breakfast, in accord with an unspoken agreement, everyone could have seven more minutes of shut-eye. Those were moments of bliss: after a hot meal, and with a premonition of the torturous work ahead of them—the cold, the wind, the heavy rucksacks—they allowed themselves to float away in deep slumber those precious seven minutes.

And then this bit of non-scheduled rest was over, and it was time to really get up, to "get into harness." The first up was almost invariably Vasili, followed usually by Ledenev, Khmelevsky, and Shparo. Davydov and Melnikov were the slugabeds. In order to awaken Anatoli one had to resort at times to some pretty strong words. To be fair, it must be said that he suffered from a chronic lack of sleep: the evening radio conversations, as I have mentioned, almost always lasted till midnight; the others would already be into their second dream while poor Melnikov would sit fighting off sleep by his radio.

In the mornings getting everything ready for the day's trek took up most of the time. The tent had to be taken down and packed, the antenna had to be dismantled, various items of personal and common equipment had to be evenly distributed among the rucksacks. This last was a painstaking job. Pack some small item in the wrong place and it could ruin your whole day: a poorly packed rucksack always seemed much heavier, and could cause bloody welts on the back and shoulders.

That is why the skiers took their time packing, sparing no pains getting everything just right. There was no set pattern for packing the rucksacks. Besides their own personal belongings someone would carry food products, another a cumbersome liferaft, a third the titanium frame of the tent, a fourth the radio station.

All these objects were different both in weight and dimensions, and of course they were using up supplies all the time, so every day they faced the puzzle of where to pack what. Each rucksack had to be properly centered, so that there would be not even a hint of any sharp corners. Dmitri was best at this, while the rucksack with the greatest number of protuberances was usually on Khmelevsky's back. Even in this Yuri was true to himself, considering it an insignificant detail. In his daily struggle with his poorly packed rucksack Khmelevsky was saved by his tremendous physical strength and his ability to ignore pain.

Below is a list of equipment carried by the expedition.

INDIVIDUAL EQUIPMENT

1. Kapron rucksack
2. Down jacket
3. Down sleeping bag
4. Down mittens
5. Parka
6. Thick sweater
7. Light sweater
8. Thick shirt
9. Long underwear
10. Woolen tights
11. Twill trousers
12. Woolen cap
13. Woolen ski mask
14. Fur hat
15. Fur mittens
16. Canvas mittens
17. Arktika woolen gloves
18. Woolen mittens
19. Mohair scarf
20. Ordinary socks

21. Thin woolen socks
22. Thick woolen socks
23. Fur socks
24. Ski boots with insoles
25. Leggings
26. Polyurethane foam mattress
27. Skis
28. Ski poles
29. Compass
30. Knife
31. Sunglasses
32. Wristwatch
33. Belt
34. Notebook
35. Bowl, cup, spoon
36. Kapron sack for personal belongings
37. Flare gun with cartridges
38. Waterproof bag
39. Polyethylene bags
40. Head-mounted flashlight

GROUP EQUIPMENT

1. Tent (4.2kg)
2. Tent frame (3 kg)
3. Snow brush
4. Saw with case
5. Tool kit
6. Ice ax
7. Two primus stoves (1.2 kg each)
8. Funnel for gasoline
9. Cooker with case
10. Pot stand
11. Heat screen
12. Ten-liter jerry can (8.5 kg)
13. Five-liter jerry can (4.5 kg)
14. Two-and-a-half-liter jerry can (2.3 kg)
15. Alcohol flask
16. Matches
17. Toilet paper
18. Kapron parka
19. Kapron trousers
20. Kapron socks
21. Thermometer
22. Anemometer
23. Barometer
24. Carbine (3.7 kg), twenty cartridges
25. LAS liferaft with case (12.7 kg)
26. MLAS liferaft with case (2.5 kg)
27. Oars with case (1.5 kg)
28. Pump
29. Repair kit for liferafts
30. Spare ski
31. Spare ski pole
32. Ski bindings (one set)

33. Night and daytime signal flares
34. Flare gun
35. Flares
36. Head-mounted flashlight
37. Flashlight batteries
38. Large flashlight
39. Batteries for large flashlight
40. Movie camera (3.4 kg)
41. Film (3.4 kg)
42. Film bag
43. Exposure meter
44. Sack for film
45. Narrow film cameras (three)
46. Wide film cameras (two)
47. Black-and-white film
48. Color film
49. Wide black-and-white film
50. Wide color film
51. Alarm clock
52. Signal mirror
53. USSR flag
54. Flag of the "Burevestnik" Sports Society
55. Thin rope
56. Thick rope
57. Antenna struts
58. Radio equipment (19 kg)
59. Navigational instruments (10 kg)
60. First-aid kit

At this point in the journey they were all very tired. Indeed, there are few people who have ever experienced such fatigue. For two months already, day in and day out, they had steadfastly guided their skis toward the Pole. They had overcome the bitter cold of the first days, the southerly ice drift, the ridges of punishing hummocks, the treacherous patches of open water. . . . What else had the Arctic in store for them?

Rakhamnov had developed the ability to sleep on the go, while Melnikov, while skiing across the ice, once fell asleep so soundly that he even dreamed.

They had finally picked up the northerly drift they had hoped for, a sort of tailwind, and weather was no longer so bitter. The worst hummocks seemed behind them now, and the sun shone round the clock. Yet there was a new enemy lying in wait for them, an enemy that had not been encountered on previous expeditions, one perhaps more dangerous than any of the rest. Its name was nervous overstress.

The history of polar exploration abounds with examples of how people in difficult situations, separated from the civilized world, stopped trusting each other and began quarreling. At the end of the last century a small vessel, the *Belgique,* spent an entire winter off the shores of Antarctica. Due to the unbearable atmosphere that had developed among the crew, two of its members went mad. An eyewitness describes life on board the vessel in these words: "The smoky cabins poorly illuminated by the flickering light of kerosene lamps became infested with disenchantment, depression, irritation—they deprive the people of mutual trust and poison the atmosphere." This was a real case of "expeditionary madness," a disease about which not a single word is to be found in the medical literature.

One more example: the Norwegian explorer Nansen, in his try for the North Pole was accompanied by the navigator of the ship *Fram,* Jalmar Fredrick Johansen. Their heroic journey lasted many months. When finally they realized they would never reach the Pole, these courageous men turned their dogsleds back. It took them almost a year and a half to reach the mainland, during which time they fed upon raw walrus and bear meat. However, the greatest trial turned out to be that from a certain moment these friends stopped talking to each other. A feeling of mutual hostility separated them, alienated them. Only once or twice a week, in strictly official form, did they address each other. Nansen and Johansen only recently had been comrades, people who today would be described as psychologically compatible.

Experts believe that more often than not conflicting situations in an isolated group develop when a man's "brakes don't hold," when he ceases to control his behavior. The disruption of inhibiting processes in extreme conditions is caused by nervous stress. A famous American explorer of the Antarctic, Admiral Richard Byrd, once pointed out that life at a polar station is limited to four walls, and that everything you do, say, and even think becomes known to everyone. Here you will fool no one for long. Sooner or later, the character of a man has to come to the surface.

In his radio interview, Shparo was by no means trying to be evasive when he said that everything was all right with regard to psychological compatibility within the group. That was the truth; after all, the men had spent many years becoming accustomed to one another, and had spent many days and nights eating together out of a single pot. Nevertheless, a certain level of tension did develop between some members of the expedition. In the opinion of most psychologists this is inevitable; the doctors link it to the fatigue the men experienced at the half-way mark.

The first signal was the argument between Melnikov and Shishkarev I have already mentioned. Vasili was really sore at Anatoli, although the latter seems to have had greater reason to take offense. First Shishkarev stopped talking to Melnikov for about four days. Then he rather demonstratively stopped helping him dismantle and pack the antenna in the mornings, a job he previously performed quite eagerly. Finally, he seemed continually to be finding fault with him.

On April 19 Anatoli did not feel well and was lagging behind the group. "It seems like they pulled the rod out of my back," he complained. "My muscles feel like cotton." Once, while clambering over a ridge of hummocks, he slipped and fell into soft snow. It felt like a fluffy quilt. His eyes closed and soon he was fast asleep. Dmitri found him twenty minutes later half covered with snow. It was not easy to get him awake.

Melnikov did not reach the next stop until the other men were ready to move on. Barely managing to stay on his feet, he stumbled up to the group and flopped on the snow. Vasili seemed to have been waiting for this moment. "Time's up," he ordered. "On your feet." And he began hoisting his rucksack. Even Dmitri could not restrain himself at the sight: "Come on," he said to Vasili, "take it easy."

Shparo himself had carried on a running feud with Ledenev that left a very unpleasant impression on the rest of the team. It had been brewing from the very first days of April, and the reason lay in their different approaches to the tactics of moving over the ice. As a rule Vladimir always tried to be the front man. Whenever he came across a crack splitting the ice perpendicular to their course, he went to the left, i.e. the west, to find a crossing. Dmitri rebuked him, saying they should move eastward whenever possible. The next time they encountered such a crevice, Ledenev veered to the right, only to again trigger the chief's dissatisfaction: "You act without thinking. It would be much more convenient to bypass this crevice from the west." The exchange which followed ended when Ledenev, having never even turned around, went on again to blaze the trail. But now, whenever he came up to a crevice, he would simply come to a halt and wait until the rest of the team pulled up. Shparo came up to him.

"Well, why are we standing?"

"A crevice," replied the imperturbable Ledenev, pointing forward with his ski pole.

"So you want to hold up the group intentionally!"

"I simply do not know what idea will enter your head next," Vladimir roared back at him.

The team traveled the rest of the day without saying a single word. It was only in the tent, before going to sleep, that Shparo returned to the incident.

"We have many ways of influencing careless people,"

he said in a cold tone. "I'll resort to the most lenient. I shall probably record today's incident in the logbook."

No one said a word to this. Everyone realized that trouble was brewing, and that any careless word here might cause irreparable damage.

The next eight to ten days changed the atmosphere very little. Dmitri quarreled with Shishkarev on a similar issue, and from that moment on the cheerful person whose birthday had recently been celebrated retreated into himself. Usually he was last in line, and composed ironic ditties about the chief of the expedition. Vasili recited his verses only to Khmelevsky. Yuri usually complimented the rhymes, but did not approve of the poet himself. "You're placing your personal interests above the group's," he rebuked him. "It does not behoove a grown-up to grumble as you do." To this Vasili replied: "I have the right to feel offended. It'll be easier now if I stay in the shadows."

At night and at lunchtime the seven practically stopped talking to each other. They simply sat on their rucksacks and gazed apathetically at their surroundings. They simply did not care; they seemed wrapped in a cloak of indifference.

Strangely, however, their rate of progress toward the Pole hit an all-time high: some days they covered more than thirty kilometers.

Two men then came to the fore, practically unnoticed—Khmelevsky and Melnikov. It was they who maneuvered delicately around the sharp corners of whatever conflicts flared up; they could defuse a tense situation by joking about it or putting forth a compromise. Throughout this trying period they carried themselves very evenly and benevolently.

Anatoli worked hard at improving the psychological climate. First he tried to restore normal relations with Vasili. Then, in quiet, confidential talks with the various team members, he convinced them they should be more tolerant toward Dmitri and his slips if he should make them in the future.

"You've got to understand," Anatoli pointed out to his comrades, "that Shparo is more tired than all of us. For many months now he hasn't had more than four or five hours of sleep a day. Besides his rucksack, he shoulders the great responsibility for the life of each one of us. I myself do not understand how he is still on his feet."

Melnikov also managed to convince the men that Dmitri should be exempt from KP duty. Like an expert physician Anatoli gradually and painlessly healed the wounds inflicted upon the expedition by these quarrels.

No one was really surprised to find Melnikov cast in this role; his qualities of loyalty, empathy, and quiet strength were evident from the day he joined up. The expedition's need for a professional radio operator had emerged quite acutely at the beginning of the 1970s. A person had to be found who was a thorough professional in radio communications, who by virtue of his physical strength and willpower would be able to participate in the toughest polar treks, and who above all should be "captivated by the Arctic, by the North Pole." This combination proved not so easy to come by.

One day Shparo was advised to meet a young man he was told might "fit the bill." The man's name—Melnikov—meant nothing to anyone. He was employed as a radio engineer. Rumor had it he was an inveterate hiker. Shparo and Melnikov met one day in September 1971, in front of the Revolution Square subway station, and became so engrossed in conversation that they did not notice that three hours had passed.

Anatoli's outward appearance impressed Dmitri immediately: tall, strong, very calm. Confidence and reliability radiated from him. There he was just as clear as day, without mannerisms—a straightforward man.

They strolled along the boulevards of Moscow, gradually getting to know each other. Melnikov's story was as plain as he himself. He was born and grew up in Moscow, in an overcrowded communal apartment not far from the Kursky Railway Terminal. His father was a truck driver, his mother a charwoman. As a boy he was a notorious mischief-maker, and he lived in a district where it was considered honorable to get your point across with your fists. He barely finished sixth grade. And he would probably have had a tough time in life, if in December of 1955 a man had not come to their school and introduced himself as a traveling instructor from the Bauman Young Pioneers House. When he invited Anatoli and his schoolmates to go on a ski hike outside Moscow, the entire class volunteered. That was Melnikov's first journey, and it changed his entire life.

Now in the evenings, instead of rushing out to meet the boys in the street, he hurried to the Young Pioneers House. Every weekend he went hiking with his new friends, and he eagerly awaited the summer so he could devote his vacation to journeying. Upon finishing school, Anatoli had no doubts as to his future profession: he would become a geologist. His passion for hiking was so great that he could not imagine himself not traveling, without a rucksack on his back, without the evening campfires and tents. It turned out that this little boy from a communal apartment was an incorrigible adventurer.

However, Anatoli failed to pass his entrance exams to the Geological Prospecting Institute. He then hired up as an ordinary worker with a topographical expedition and a year later was called up into the army. Quickly rising to the rank of sergeant in the signal corps, he was sent to the city of Norilsk, above the Arctic Circle, for a three-year tour of duty. After demobilization he enrolled at the Institute of Communications, having passed his entrance exams with flying colors, and subsequently earned the

202

highest marks in his class. Not at all surprisingly, during his first summer vacation he began what was to be a whole series of journeys by trekking to the Onega Peninsula.

Listening to him, Dmitri realized that standing before him was exactly the man they were looking for.

"Anatoli," Shparo said, "we are preparing for a journey across Long Strait. After that we may go further north. I believe you could participate in our expedition as a radio operator."

Melnikov was silent for a moment, and then calmly looking out of his blue eyes said, "I'm ready."

On Long Strait he managed to bail me out of a lot of trouble. When I fell ill and it became clear we had to call for a helicopter immediately, our radio station went suddenly on the blink. Night fell, I was feeling worse, and still no contact with the mainland. (At that time our equipment was weak, and communications with the mainland were unreliable.) For the rest of my life I will remember that night spent in the middle of Long Strait. It was extremely dark, and I was shaking with the chills. No one was sleeping. The others switched on their flashlights and held them so as to give Melnikov as much light as possible as he spent the entire night repairing the radio. From touching cold metal his fingers became swollen and cracked, and eventually began to bleed. No one said a word; they all just sat there looking hopefully in his direction. It was morning before Anatoli finally found the transistor that had been knocked out, and was able to replace it. He switched on his set and almost instantly made contact with the radio operator at the closest polar station. "Information received, helicopter on its way."

After the journey across Long Strait, Melnikov seemed to drop out of the picture for a while. He stopped participating in training sessions and general get-togethers, and did not show any interest in future expeditions. Why? He himself now explains it this way: "I didn't think the idea of trekking to the North Pole was feasible. There was plenty of talk about it, but very little was being done—and that irritated me."

Shparo, however, did not want to rule him out. He would ring up Melnikov and inform him, as if nothing had happened, "Tomorrow we meet at Ledenev's place on the subject of equipment." Or: "We're heading for the Taimyr Peninsula. You could come along if you wanted to." In the end Anatoli gave in: by the summer of 1974 he was again with us.

One day he tried to explain the reasons that had instilled in him his passion for exploration: "A calm existence puts me to sleep. Tight situations—and there are plenty on any expedition—get me going. This is real living. A man's best qualities seem to come to the fore during grueling treks, in a crowded tent, beside the campfire at night. People seem to open up before each other, and you can see their goodness, their honesty, their nobility."

Northerners, who are very good at sizing people up, are quick to single out Anatoli: "Your radio operator will never let you down."

Prone to self-analysis, Melnikov clearly realizes his weaknesses. "I am too passive," he says. "Rather than fight, I would prefer a compromise. I am not a leader, yet I'm ready to uphold my opinion to the end. And whenever all the others display weakness, I do too. Perhaps I am simply one block of a foundation."

Just how much his authority is valued in the group can be seen from the following: before starting out for the Pole, Melnikov was unanimously elected Communist Party organizer of the expedition. Through all the years since he joined the group, no one had any doubts as to who would be the radio operator in the team heading for the Pole. During these years scores of men passed through the expedition—participated in treks and training sessions, helped design and construct equipment, conducted historical research in libraries and archives—yet no one was a worthy contender for Melnikov.

The turning point in the mood of the group came at the end of April. The men seemed to awaken from a horrible nightmare. Once again their relations were marked by the usual sincerity, trust, joyfulness, and openness to one another. The efforts of the men themselves were largely responsible for this change, but it was prompted also by their success in moving northward. Nor should the long radio discussions conducted with the group by psychologist Mikhail Novikov, who flew in from Moscow to NP-24, be discounted.

Once again the dispatches from the ski team radiated vitality and humor. Against the background of his comrades' laughter, Ledenev, in an interview for Radio Moscow, praised the Arctic as a wonderful place for summer vacations.

"Dear friends!" he deadpanned. "Summer vacations are just around the corner. Take a look at the map, and choose any destination you wish. But I can tell you about a wonderful spot on the globe where the sun never sets, the air is pure, and there is plenty of seawater for swimming."

Vasili composed a verse about each of his six comrades, and there was not a trace of dejection or rancor to be found. Even Dmitri became less irritable. At the beginning of May he sent a dispatch to *Komsomolskaya Pravda:* "On April 29 we set a record: we covered approximately forty kilometers in a single day! The weather yesterday was unusual: a white mist covered the ice, obscuring the sky, and this, more than ever before, made us feel the inconvenience of traveling by compass alone. The arrow would point northward, then suddenly it would veer to the west, and then almost reluctantly it would return to its former position.

"From past experience we felt that the sunny weather would soon return. And lo and behold, at 1300 the next day the brilliant sun emerged through the mist, low on the horizon over the Arctic desert of ice. During our lunch stop we were able to determine our latitude, but after our meal and a nap the sun just as suddenly disappeared, and once again we found ourselves submerged in a medium like milky muslin. At 1800, as if playing hide-and-seek with the navigators, the red circle of the sun popped out again in the west. Khmelevsky and Rakhmanov nabbed the luminary in the eyepiece of the theodolite, and then once again it vanished.

"Variable wind, variable cloudiness, changeable weather—that characterizes April 29. On the following day there was not even a trace of cloud cover. Our spirits rose because the third airdrop of food and fuel was scheduled for 2000 hours that day. In order to save time, the tent was not set up at lunchtime. At 1600 visibility once again dropped, and the wind turned more sharply to the north. At 1800 we were to go on the air to inform the pilots of our position. That meant camp had to be pitched at 1730.

"The icefields we were crossing were small and very hummocky, absolutely unsuitable for an airdrop. We were really worried. Melnikov was especially nervous—he was afraid he might be late going on the air. At 1700 our route was blocked by a channel of open water four meters wide. Heading eastward we found an icefloe that served as a pontoon bridge letting us across. I clambered up a hummock and just ahead of us could make out two large fields surrounded by a fence of hummocks.

"Without hurrying we set up camp. Anatoli went on the air, and fifteen minutes later a plane took off from NP-24.

"Visibility worsened as the wind velocity increased; our nervousness heightened. We had a reserve of gasoline

206

and food, and we could have continued on our way for several more days. Still, the situation was quite tense.

"We spotted the aircraft but could not hear it. The strong north wind carried away the roar of the engines, as the IL-14 was flying in from the south. It emerged as a huge and powerful bird over a ridge of hummocks some six hundred meters from our tent. Then the containers came sailing down suspended from their parachutes. But here we were in for a surprise: on the ice the strong wind filled the parachutes and our containers went zipping across the snow to the south. Fortunately we had foreseen this: four of our men stood ready at the edge of the hummocks. The shrouds became snagged in the hummocks, and they pounced on the billowing nylon.

"The wind was blowing very strongly. Dragging into the tent what we needed most, we no longer ventured outside. Vasili was the last to crawl into the tent: 'The wind is gusting between eighteen and twenty meters per second, northerly direction; temperature, minus seven,' he reported.

"On May Day we held a meeting near our tent. We congratulated each other on the holiday. Vadim fired a salute from his carbine. Ledenev and Rakhmanov took some pictures. Meanwhile, the blizzard raged on.

"On May 3 our coordinates were 85°01' north latitude, 157°30' east longitude."

The Pole Is Ours!

On May 10 we spent a great deal of time at headquarters discussing how to organize the celebration at the Pole upon completion of the expedition. Who should be present? What should be left at the Pole as a token of the conquest? Finally, the chief of headquarters got the bright idea of placing these questions before the readers of *Komsomolskaya Pravda*—let them make suggestions and proposals. An article encouraging submissions appeared in the next edition and triggered an avalanche of letters.

They offered many sensible suggestions: raise the state flag of the USSR at the North Pole and next to it the flag of the Papanin expedition; leave at the Pole an airtight, unsinkable container with notes in both Russian and English; place at the Pole portraits of Russian explorers who have perished in the struggle with the Arctic. In addition, many naive and very touching letters came from children.

Among them were the following suggestions: carry out a tasting of a new brand of ice cream called "Northern Lights"; build a house at the Pole and place in it a dove (the symbol of peace), Misha (the bearcub mascot of the Moscow Olympics), and a doll (as a token marking the International Year of the Child); sell hot meat pies during the ceremony; hold a world championship annually (the team to reach the Pole on skis in the shortest possible time would be the winner); upon reaching the Pole, the team should go for a swim and drink their fill of water; build a monument in honor of the seven daring skiers at the finishing point. And so it went.

Komsomolskaya Pravda also received heartfelt greetings and congratulations from Thor Heyerdahl, the famous Norwegian explorer; John Henning, Director of the Royal Geographical Society of Great Britain; Professor Robert Maclay of Australia; A. Mrkos, Director of the Astronomical Observatory in Czechoslovakia; and Naomi Uemura, the Japanese explorer.

During a radio talk with the *Salyut-6–Soyuz-32* space complex, Soviet cosmonauts Vladimir Lyakhov and Valeri Ryumin reported that they were following the progress of the ski team and wished them a speedy victory.

"I salute the daring trek of your scientific-sporting expedition," Ivan Papanin, twice Hero of the Soviet Union, radioed the ice camp. "You are tackling a great mission. I believe you will cope with it; I have faith in you."

The USSR Communications Ministry issued two separate envelopes and a postcard depicting the participants of the expedition. On the day the team reached the Pole, the Main Post Office in Moscow used a special memorial mark for canceling postage stamps.

The expedition was coming down the homestretch.

Headquarters agreed to Labutin's proposal that he be relocated at NP-24. In the middle of May, with the help of Oleg Obukhov, who was appointed permanent head-quarters representative in Chersky, Labutin, Deyev, and part of the powerful radio equipment were airlifted to the drifting station. A local ham operator volunteered to monitor the radio set on Kotelny, and NP-24 became the main base for the expedition.

Those days I noticed that subconsciously I was acting in empathy with the ski group. For instance, realizing that my comrades were giving their all amid the ice at the top of the world, I could not allow myself to be idle, to have a good time, or to sleep more than six hours a day. Even my little car seemed peppier, as if the mood of its driver was transmitted to valves and pistons.

On May 15, at six in the morning, I zipped over to Vnukovo Airport to pass on letters and the latest newspapers for the expedition. The last scheduled airdrop was to take place in three days. As I drove along the practically empty highway at that early hour, I realized with a pang of regret that soon this undertaking, into which so much effort and spirit had been poured, would be over. I was sorry these days were running out—days filled with anxiety, hard work, and concern, but days which would never return. Soon, very soon, the project that had been so much a part of our lives would recede into the past.

The month of May brought an early summer to Moscow. But north of the 85th parallel it besieged the skiers with blizzards and white mists. The temperature hovered around minus twenty. The skiers were especially tormented by the white mists, when snow and air become indistinguishable and shadows disappear, destroying any sense of perspective. In May this white mist hung in the air practically every day. It was an impenetrable white night. And if you removed your sunglasses, snow blindness would set in almost instantly.

I remember a nasty trick the white mist played on us once on Severnaya Zemlya. During one of the stops Boris

Lyubimov noticed a huge cliff ahead, apparently jutting out of a glacier. A heated argument developed as to how many kilometers distant it was.

"Two," I pronounced with authority. "To be exact: two kilometers, four hundred meters."

I was sure I had a good eye.

"No, not two kilometers," objected Boris. "I'd say it was about five hundred meters."

Yuri, always the sly one, had said nothing so far. He pulled out a map and scrutinized it carefully. There was no cliff designated on the map, and after giving it some thought Yuri cautiously said that perhaps there was really nothing there. Dmitri supported him.

I scoffed at them: "You no longer believe your eyes. Just look at that huge cliff. Perhaps there are birds nesting there. We'll make our next stop right at its foot."

"It would be great to get some eggs for an omelette," added Boris.

We got up and continued on our way, Boris in the lead. After ten steps he stopped and turned around, looking baffled and a bit shame-faced. When the rest caught up he pointed ahead with his ski pole. Some three steps in front of him lay a small stone the size of a hen's egg.

"Well, can you beat that!" I said in utter amazement. "So that's our cliff!"

The psychologists took a keen interest in stories about the white mist and offered the following observations: "In your diaries you noted that such weather irritated you considerably. We noticed also that your entries for those days are very meager and monotonous. They seemed to reflect your fatigue and irritation. American psychologists once performed the following experiment: they gave students an interesting lecture in an absolutely white classroom. Most of the students fell asleep. The conclusion was obvious: when the number of external stimuli drops sharply, when a man is surrounded by a monotonous, doleful atmosphere, his work capacity and creativity decrease. In another experiment, a professor of physics and mathematics, a learned and self-disciplined scholar, placed himself in an absolutely white chamber and tried to do his work. Of course, he produced nothing. Now, that chamber and the situation you found yourselves in during the white mists have much in common. They have a similar effect on the mind."

With the onset of warm weather, a surprising thing occurred: the mood of the skiers soured almost as it had in the recent cold stretch. When I say "warm" I mean that the temperature was a mere minus ten or fifteen. But dressed as they were, traversing the hummocks with a heavy pack caused sweat to run down their faces; the thirst was tormenting, and they felt like throwing off their thick parkas. Yet it was necessary to be cautious while experimenting with clothing: first of all, the cold weather might suddenly return, and, second, even given the warm weather as a constant, sudden gusts of moist wind, coming into contact with their sweating bodies, might easily provoke pneumonia.

Nevertheless, they did discard certain items of their wardrobe. For instance, their fur socks and mittens. Certainly they felt sorry to leave on the ice items that had served them well, yet no one wanted to keep on lugging them: each extra gram of weight in the rucksack made its presence known through bloody welts on the shoulders.

Incidentally, in the attempt to make his rucksack lighter, Vadim was more successful than anyone else. Every day he would chuck out another of his personal belongings, and very boldly used scissors to snip off parts of his sweater, his storm suit, his leggings. Once he asked, "What freezes more—your back or your belly?" He answered the question himself: "Your back, of course." Upon which he snipped out a huge circle in the front of his thick sweater. "See that? The sweater is much lighter

213

now," Vadim explained. And when the night rapidly began to grow shorter, giving way to twilight, Davydov suggested pitching the candles. But at this point Ledenev flared up: "Leave the candles alone!" he barked.

"Vladimir," said Vadim peaceably, "it'll be easier for you. The candles weigh at least a hundred grams."

But Ledenev was adamant: "I don't tell you what to do with your first-aid kit, so you leave my repair kit alone."

The candles, together with tools, screws, wire, insulating tape, needles, pins, and dozens of other items, were part of the repair kit. The future was to prove Ledenev correct in this dispute; in May the candles were needed in absolutely unforeseen circumstances. Not only were the men worn out, but so also was the extra-strong synthetic fabric of the rucksacks. It began to tear. And in order to repair it, there was nothing better than a burning candle to melt and seal the edge of the fabric before sewing it.

Robert Peary once remarked that in the Arctic explorers always welcome bitter cold because milder temperatures and a snowfall always mean open water and consequent delays. The skiers could readily agree.

On May 5, after a three-day blizzard, Shparo crawled out of the tent in the morning and clambered up a tall hummock. The view that opened up before his eyes was astounding: the camp was surrounded by numerous lakes, each connected to the others by a network of channels. The blizzard had broken up the ice fields. Soon the others had joined Dmitri on the hummock.

"Arctic high water," Khmelevsky announced as he surveyed the scene.

"The Venice of the 85th parallel," added Rakhmanov, being inclined toward romantic comparisons.

But Dmitri was downcast. "If this keeps up we'll be lucky to reach the Pole by the end of the year."

"What's the rush?" Ledenev said, almost sadly. "So we finish our trek to the Pole; then what? We return home. Will we ever again find anything as interesting, as gripping? What we're doing right now, right here, will never be repeated. We must cherish these days."

"You're right, my friend," Shparo said quietly. "I think of that more and more often. The best days of our lives. . . . But even so, we must make haste. By the end of May we must reach the Pole without fail."

Crossing these water barriers—cracks, channels, lakes—required a set of rules governing their behavior around water. "The main thing is discipline, caution, and mutual aid," Dmitri kept repeating.

As a rule the crossings went smoothly. Only on rare occasions did anyone fall in, and even then only up to the waist or the knees. There were other insignificant mishaps. Rakhmanov, for instance, once came up to the edge of a crack, but did not realize what he was standing on—not ice, but a cantilever of packed snow, jutting out over the water. At that moment the snow broke loose and went crashing into the water, but Vladimir managed just in the nick of time to fall backward. A close call. . . . Then there was another crack, this one covered by a thin layer of fresh ice, almost black. Under the weight of a person such ice behaves like fabric stretched tautly across a frame. The first to cross was Ledenev. Not only is he the lightest member of the team; he was also carrying the movie camera and wished to film this tense moment from the other side. Then Vasili, Dmitri, and Yuri crossed. Next was Vadim, notorious for being too independent: instead of following in their tracks he veered slightly to the left. Instantly the tips of his skis dipped into the water. But nearby was a solid icefloe on which Shiskarev was backing up Davydov. Vasili grabbed the doctor by his hands and yanked him out of the water in a split second.

One further incident. In the three-meter-thick pack

215

ice they came across a narrow crevice. One by one, the skiers calmly stepped across it, and continued on their way. All of a sudden there was a loud noise behind them, a muffled shout, and some strong language. It seems Melnikov had fallen asleep on the go and somehow had tumbled into the crevice head first. His skis now straddled the crevice, while Anatoli himself was suspended upside down like the letter "V." When the others reached him, Melnikov was still not fully awake.

"Give me your leg!" he shouted.

The men could not contain their laughter: "Why a leg? How about a hand?"

"What's the difference!" Melnikov roared. "Just give me something to get out of here. I can't hold on much longer."

How he got himself into such an awkward position no one, including himself, could explain. For a long time after, they recalled the episode with a smile.

The group encountered a especially great deal of water on May 8 and 9. But thanks to their confidence, their competence, and their daring, their progress was still quite good. On May 9 they crossed the 86th parallel. Only four degrees now separated them from their coveted goal. That evening Shparo reminded them all that today was Victory Day, the day commemorating the Soviet defeat of Nazi Germany in World War II.

"Yes," declared Rakhmanov, "but today is not only Victory Day; it is also the anniversary of an event related to the conquest of the Pole."

Ledenev perked up his ears. "What event?" he asked.

"May 9." Dmitri said, thinking out loud. "What do you have in mind?"

The obliging Rakhmanov needed no more prodding: "Exactly thirty years ago today the first parachutists landed at the Pole."

"Why, you're right!" exclaimed Dmitri, disappointed

216

he had not remembered this himself. "Volovich and Medvedev were the parachutists."

"Correct," Vladimir said in confirmation.

"Wait a minute." Yuri seemed to be excited. "Could that be the same Volovich?"

"The very same."

"Can you beat that! I didn't know that about him. Does anyone know the details?"

In a nutshell, here is the story: in the winter of 1949 a young doctor by the name of Vitali Volovich was urgently summoned to the Head Office of the North Coast Route Administration. That historic building on Razin Street was known to many Muscovites at that time: this was the headquarters of the famous Arctic expeditions, of the first Heroes of the Soviet Union, the legendary polar explorers, pilots, and scientists.

Somewhat intimidated, Vitali mounted the wide staircase to the second floor and headed for the reception room. The secretary pointed to the heavy oak door. "They're waiting for you," he said. In the spacious office Volovich became even more dismayed. Turning their attention from a map of the Arctic, Mikhail Vodopyanov, Ilya Mazuruk, Ivan Cherevichny—famous polar explorers all—looked toward the young doctor with interest.

"Would you like to participate in an air expedition in the higher latitudes?" one of them asked.

At that time such a question was equivalent to asking a person today whether he would like to fly into outer space.

"You would have to perform a doctor's duties in unusual circumstances. For instance, if it became necessary, would you be able to parachute onto a drifting icefloe?"

"Even without a parachute," replied Vitali, inspired by the unexpected proposal. "But seriously, I have already made seventy-four parachute jumps."

"That's why we asked you."

VLADIMIR SNEGIREV

In March heavy cargo planes delivered the expedition's equipment to the ice and they began studying the central part of the Arctic basin. As polar explorers rarely fall ill, the doctor did not have much to do.

Finally, working up his courage, Volovich addressed the chief of the expedition: "Papanin's men consolidated our achievements in Arctic exploration at the Pole. Soviet aircraft have made quite a number of landings at the earth's axis. What would you say if we draped the Pole with a parachute?"

The chief squinted his eyes, gave a little snort . . . and said nothing.

Several days passed. Their investigations at higher latitudes were coming to an end. One after another the planes took off for home. Then, on the morning of May 9, Volovich was summoned to the chief's tent.

"Today you can make your dream come true. You'll make the jump together with an experienced parachutist, Andrei Medvedev."

The sun was shining brightly in the region of the Pole. The twin-engine aircraft, flying at an altitude of six hundred meters, zeroed in on the one point from which it is south in all directions. Though there was no need for it, Volovich kept checking the carefully packed parachutes and fumbled with the straps. Medvedev, an experienced parachutist with a Master of Sports rating, a man who had made many jumps into water, into forests and mountains, a paratrooper who had been dropped behind enemy lines in wartime, was also not feeling quite himself. No one had yet opened a parachute over the North Pole.

The siren started to wail: time to get ready for the jump. The flight engineer, cursing under his breath, was still fiddling around with the door locks. Either he was nervous, or the metal door had jammed in the cold. "As you were!" ordered the chief, and waved the parachutists back to their seats. The plane banked steeply, and went back for another pass.

218

THE POLE IS OURS!

Finally the door was opened. The parachutists got up and readied themselves for the jump. The feeling of anxiety gave way to a feeling of internal self-control and confidence. The time was 1305. Then the siren wailed again, and Andrei, and after him Vitali, kicked off smartly and went plummeting into the void.

The daring jump immediately made the young doctor popular with other polar explorers. They invited him to work at NP-2 and NP-3. After that, his life was a constant round of adventures and exploits. Studying problems connected with the survival of human beings in harsh environments, he drifted in a lifeboat in the Indian Ocean, hacked his way through the jungles of Southeast Asia, and conducted unique experiments in taiga and desert. For many Soviet cosmonauts—those on the *Vostok* and *Voskhod* spaceships—he was the first earthling they saw upon their return from outer space: Volovich descended to them by parachute. He is the author of a unique and very interesting book, *The Survival of Aircraft Crews After Forced Landings*. In it, he refers to the experience of the *Komsomolskaya Pravda* permanent expedition. Khmelevsky had on many occasions discussed the scientific programs of our Arctic journeys with him, but knew nothing of his earliest exploits.

For a long time that evening the ski team did not fall asleep. From recollections about Volovich they went on to discuss their own expedition. Until recently they had avoided discussing the social significance of their trek. For them everything was perfectly clear, but it was possible they might be misunderstood. Would their expedition be properly assessed by other people—those concerned with the Arctic and those with no relation to it whatever; young people and the elderly; avid hikers and those who never journey further than the corner store? The subject first came up when, in one of the containers from the last airdrop, they found a newspaper with one of Vasili Peskov's articles on the expedition. The article was headlined "They Are Going." Everyone read it several times over.

But now once again Dmitri fished the article out of his pocket.

"I'd like to remind you of the press's opinion," he said, and began reading: "Why are they going? 'Why?' This question is as old as mankind. There was always someone journeying across the world, dooming himself to hardships and even death, while someone sitting in the cozy warmth, whether in a cave around a campfire or in front of a TV set, asked 'Why?' No one remembers those who asked the question. But history remembers those who journeyed. Who are they? They are a multitude. Columbus, Magellan, Gagarin, Armstrong. Thanks to the efforts of a whole legion of other daring explorers they discovered continents, islands, depths, straits, Poles, sea routes; they conquered mountains, mapped the minutest details of the earth, explored caves, ocean currents, and discovered ore deposits. And, finally, man looked down at the earth from cold outer space. None of this could have been achieved sitting on a rock near home or in a soft armchair. Someone had to go. Is it proper to recall the names of these famous pathfinders as we reflect on the polar journey of these seven men? I think it is. It is proper because in challenging the unknown man has always subjected himself to a test of willpower, of his physical and moral possibilities. And in this sense Semyon Dezhnev, Captain Cook, Przhevalsky, Nansen, and Valeri Chkalov stand shoulder to shoulder. Amid the hustle and bustle of everyday life, in those moments when we pause and look over our shoulders, we must have models we can look up to and say: 'Yes, that man can do it.' It is very important for humankind to have models of valor and endurance."

"Well, here he really laid it on thick," Shishkarev sarcastically interrupted. "Placing us on the same plane with Columbus, Magellan, Nansen. . . ."

"I think Peskov makes his point quite convincingly," Dmitri cut him off. "But I haven't finished reading." He continued.

"It seems that mankind as a whole needs some confirmation of unflagging strength and dauntless spirit. Perhaps this explains the steadily growing number of expeditions and journeys by boat, raft, air balloon, wagon, dogsled, and camel. And this is not to be scoffed at. Francis Chichester, the elderly Englishman who sailed around the world alone in his yacht, was knighted in his native land. Thor Heyerdahl became more than just a national hero of Norway; he became the idol of young people the world over. Could civilization have dispensed with those journeys? Of course. Yet we must agree that there is still a need for someone, somewhere, to put himself to the test, to keep on moving despite all obstacles, so that in this age of machines we do not lose faith in human valor, in human endurance, in the ability to transcend one's limitations. So that we will be able to say: 'Yes, a man can do it.' "

"Well said!" exclaimed Khmelevsky. "Yet, I wonder what percentage of mankind shares that opinion. If even a half, I would say that's good."

"What do you mean, a half?" Vasili objected. "To the majority of mankind it is useless to explain why we are going to the Pole. For instance, my sister writes in her letter: 'The fact that you are conquering the ice to reach the North Pole will not make our harvest in Kazakhstan any better.' The majority will not understand us."

"You're wrong," Melnikov said. "I am of a better opinion of mankind. And your sister, well, she takes after you."

"Here is what I think," Davydov ventured. "If the ordinary man in the street, who does not always read the newspapers, says, 'Well, I really don't know why those boys had to go to the Pole, but in general they had a tough time, and they came through the ordeal with flying colors'—if he says that, then I think everything is okay."

At about the time I was driving out to Vnukovo Airport with their mail, my friends out on the ice decided to make a real spurt northward that day and had planned to go twelve legs. They had a slight tailwind, and their mood was quite jocular. "We've entered the pre-Pole area," announced Melnikov. Suddenly, right after the hummocks, they came up against open water. "It's like what happens in the forest," Dmitri explained later. "You come out of a grove to the shores of a lake and stand there: the trunks and crowns of the trees are reflected in the water. This lake in the polar ice reflected the white and the bluish broken tops of the hummocks."

In search of a crossing, three men veered to the right, and four to the left. A narrow spot where the banks were very close to each other was spotted to the west. They decided not to inflate the liferaft and instead threw chunks of ice and snow into the water. Taking their skis off and placing them over it, they scurried across this rickety bridge to the other side. No sooner was this risky crossing completed than the ice came to life. Both banks came crashing together, erasing the lake that had been such an obstacle only a moment before, and left in its stead a range of hummocks two meters high.

During this "Arctic high water" the team had spotted a seal: the animal cautiously exposed its dark eyes from the water and seemed to look at the humans in amazement, as if to ask, "What are you doing here?" A seal! For the first time in two months they had encountered amid these barren icefloes a living creature; they were as happy as children about it.

Soon after, the skiers came across something that left them dumbstruck. They came across the absolutely fresh tracks of a polar fox. The animal was heading from west to east. A polar fox at the 88th parallel?! How did it appear here? In any direction, it was at least a thousand kilometers to the mainland. What would it feed on up here in the barren expanses of the Arctic desert?

On their tenth leg they again encountered a stretch of open water. As inflating a liferaft meant losing time, they again resorted to their time-tested method of crossing: they threw chunks of ice and snow into the water and covered them with their skis. Vadim and Vasili, backing each other up, then scurried across this bridge to the other side. Shiskharev was especially adept at this operation, hopping and skipping across this chasm of frigid water. The rucksacks were then ferried across with the help of a kapron rope.

"Then all around us the ice groaned, squeaked, and roared," Dmitri later told me. "The ice was moving every which way." Unfortunately, this time the banks of the channel did not converge but in fact parted even further. The chunks of ice that made up our bridge seemed to hover for an instant and then, having lost their foundations, began floating away. At precisely this moment Rakhmanov was setting foot on the bridge; hardly had his foot come down than it was engulfed in water. Vladimir hesitated for a split second, and before he could make a move Melnikov had dragged him onto firm ice. The icefield, under the impact of some unknown but monstrous force, was splitting up and sailing off in different directions. Dmitri had clambered up a hummock, and was getting ready to repeat Vasili's hop, skip, and jump. However, where before there had been simply a narrow crevice, now a great river washed the shore he stood on.

The group spent the night of May 17 on a small icefloe encircled by water. It was clear they had to get off it as fast as they could. Shparo and Rakhmanov went out on ice reconnaissance patrol, and soon had a piece of good luck: they discovered an unsteady ice bridge by which they could attempt a crossing. Returning to camp, they quickly got the others onto their feet and with them managed to cross the thin ice, barely getting their skis wet.

Next they encountered a channel ten meters across, with sheer cliffs on either side. At this point the liferaft had to be inflated. Thanks to their coordinated and energetic efforts—everyone knew exactly what he had to do—in less than an hour the entire team was on the other side.

In spite of all this, they remained in high spirits. Every one of them could almost taste the victorious finish. Vadim guessed they would reach the Pole on May 26. Anatoli said May 27. Yuri was the only one who would not commit himself on this account. His intuition told him that before the curtain came down the Arctic was sure to put them through a final test of their stamina. And he was right.

It was a strange thing indeed: you might have thought that as they approached the Pole the ice would become thicker, stronger, more solid, but in reality it was just the other way around. The closer they came to their goal, the more often they encountered open water and new ice. There were practically no fields of old pack ice here, and time and again, they were confronted by ridges of fresh hummocks. The group's daily progress tailed off noticeably. On May 21 the group entered a zone of thick hummocks. And that was not all.

The day before the sun had disappeared. The sky seemed drawn over with grey cotton. From time to time a very fine and dry snow descended, driven by the wind, and settled on the ice with a slight rustling sound. The atmosphere darkened and became alarming—without the sun the navigators were unable to determine the group's coordinates or to chart a course. And in the region of the Pole it was especially important that their position be regularly and accurately pinpointed. The slightest error in calculation could steer them far from the Pole.

THE POLE IS OURS!

The sun did not appear for one day, two days, three days. It seemed the clouds would never disperse. Nature seemed to have calculated its final thrust with utmost precision: these seven skiers, who had already covered almost fifteen hundred kilometers, who were weary of the cold and the snowstorms, the hummocks and the open water, were bogged down only a couple of steps from their goal.

Yuri Khmelevsky recounts: "Back in April there were moments when I bugged my comrades: 'What are we going to do if, in the last few days before we reach the Pole, the sun disappears?' Everyone scoffed and acted as if I were an idiot. Because spring in the Arctic is invariably accompanied by sunny weather, they assumed it would be clear without letup. Though no one could accuse them of being overoptimistic, they were perhaps put off guard by the fact that so far we had not made a single navigational error.

"Then came that memorable day—May 20. The whole sky was overcast. We were marching almost blind, relying on calculations. On the fifth day I said: 'Suppose we are headed in the right direction—due north. But how are we to know when to stop—that is, the moment we reach the Pole? Because if we keep on going, it will mean we are heading southward.' Instead of a reply, there was only silence.

"When it rains, it pours. To add insult to injury, in the end everyone's skis began to break. Made of hickory, the hardest wood there is, they nevertheless had been worn down to less than half their original thickness, and could no longer stand up to the grueling punishment. Rakhmanov gave his intact skis to Vadim and myself, and somehow managed to get along on our broken ones. Vladimir probably had the most difficult time of us all. Like me, he was a navigator, and was responsible for charting our course. Those days the sun seemed to be playing tag with us: no sooner did it peak out from behind the clouds than we hurriedly came to a stop and set up our theodolite on a tripod; then, when everything was ready, the sky would again cloud over. But no sooner would we pack up and set out again than the sun would reappear, peeking out of the clouds as if laughing at us.

"Rakhmanov and I had practically no sleep at all—we were keeping constant watch for the appearance of the sun. At that time of the year, at the Pole, it was equally bright both night and day; the sun 'floated' round the clock, always at the same altitude. Vladimir was really worn out, he had grown thin, yet he was true to himself. He tried to do everything as it had to be done, and he gave his all."

Vladimir Rakhmanov.

At our New Year's parties he performed tricks with Ping-Pong balls. He would produce them from his mouth, from his ears, from other people's pockets. Hocus-pocus, there you are! Vladimir bows most modestly, yet if called upon for an encore, he is eager and obliging. Two, three encores are not too many. Here is a person who will never say no.

One day we tried to estimate the tremendous amount of social and political work Rakhmanov has taken on. He is Deputy Secretary of the Party Bureau at the Mosgidstrostahl Designing Board, where he is a mechanical engineer working on hydroelectric projects. He is Chairman of the standing production conference. He is a member of the editorial board of the wall newspaper (which always appears on schedule). He is also the organizer of amateur talent shows and photo contests and a member of the auxiliary police. All this on top of being navigator, photographer, and artist of the polar expedition.

"If I am capable of something, then I must not refuse to do it," Vladimir says quietly.

Though on the surface he may seem modest and even

shy, you must remember how on Kotelny Island, in a full gale, Rakhmanov clambered up a thin guywire to the top of the mast to untangle the antenna. No shrinking violet could ever do that.

"After all, I'm an old mountain climber," he said setting down on terra firma. "I've been scaling cliffs since the age of five."

And he was not exaggerating: our navigator in fact made his first climb when he had barely learned to walk. This is what happened. When the Soviet Union entered the Second World War, Rakhmanov was living in the small mining town of Tyrniaus, in the Northern Caucasus, where his parents worked at the local molybdenum mill. In the summer of 1942 the Fascists captured the city of Nalchik and sealed off the north of Baksan Gorge, where Tyrniaus is situated. From the southwest the town was threatened also by units of the German Alpine "Edelweiss" Division, which had already scaled Mt. Elbrus. Tyrniaus was as good as taken. The Soviet Command decided that the Germans would find an empty city, and the most experienced mountain climbers were instructed to lead everyone—babes in arms to the oldest men and women—across the high mountain passes southward into Transcaucasia.

Vladimir Rakhmanov was five years old at the time. He still remembers the ordeal. It rained for several days without letup, and then up higher it began snowing. In that white wilderness the little boy was afraid to lag behind his mother, was afraid he would get lost. He clambered up the steep inclines, clinging tightly to his mother's skirt. In her arms his mother was carrying his three-year-old brother. At night they slept, finding shelter from the icy wind amid the rocks. For food they gnawed on hard crusts of bread.

After three days, several thousand weary people (including three hundred children of preschool age) reached the valley of the Inguri River. In the Georgian town of Zugdidi they found food and warmth. From here they eventually crossed the Caspian Sea to the city of Krasnovodsk, and then left for Siberia, where they lived till the end of the war.

Thirty-five years later, Vladimir had returned to these very places—the valley of the mountain river Inguri, the Georgian town of Zugdidi—to build a hydroelectric station. During his vacation that year he and his son spent their time retracing the route he had taken during the war years. By this time Rakhmanov was already an experienced mountain climber, practically a professional alpinist, but even now he found it hard going on the steep, snow-covered slopes. He found it hard to imagine how the women, the old men, the children, had survived the ordeal those many years ago.

The Inguri hydroelectric station is not the only facility he has designed. Working in the designing bureau he has traveled far and wide. Riga, Bratsk, Votkinsk, Nizhnekamsk—everywhere he has left a bit of his labor. Rakhmanov's work in Vietnam building the K'hakba hydroelectric station earned him a citation from the People's Republic of Vietnam—Order of Labor Third Class. His attitude toward these long journeys is about the same as a housewife's attitude toward going to the local bakery. For him that is the only way to live.

Even on holidays you will rarely find Rakhmanov at home. The entire family—Vladimir, his wife, his son—get into their canoe and set off into the wilderness. Difficult journeys are no problem for him. Vladimir says little, but does a great deal: he is always helping someone, repairing things, always busy at something. And he never parts with his camera.

"Why do you participate in these hazardous journeys?" he was once asked on a television program.

As usual when attention is focused on him, Rakhmanov blushed. "A real man must always be in good shape," he said, "and for that he must have a little adventure from time to time."

"You have quite a sense of humor," the interviewer laughed.

"But I'm not joking," replied Rakhmanov. "Perhaps you have misunderstood me. A man is distinguished by his ability to 'give his all,' to press himself to his limit. In fact it is the same quality as being able to think."

In general, Rakhmanov avoids these interviews as if they were the plague. He dislikes lofty words and a big fuss. I have already mentioned that he is modest almost to a fault, and this is no act. His modesty and strength of character run very deep indeed.

I have a letter in my files. "Dear Editor!" it reads. "We have a request. Through your newspaper we would like to pass on our heartfelt greetings to one of the participants in the expedition, Vladimir Rakhmanov. We studied together for ten years, and graduated with him from the tenth grade at School No. 3 in the city of Electrostahl. In our class not a single boy was more popular than Vladimir. There were other nice boys, but he was the only one who presented us girls with white roses from his garden, though he blushed like a red rose at such moments. When he was around, all the other boys would act like chivalrous knights. And if you ever heard how he and his wife sing together to the strains of a guitar."

We have heard them singing. And time and again we have experienced the noble qualities of Vladimir Rakhmanov.

In 1976, on the way to NP-23 from Wrangel Island, he failed to protect his eyes and became snowblind, a very painful condition. Vadim gave him some eyedrops and put adhesive tape over his sunglasses to block out the light. And what do you think Vladimir did after that? He said he wanted to lead the way and even harnessed himself to the sled, which the men took turns hauling. At this point Dmitri blew his top: "Get into the tent immediately!" he roared.

And now, forty-two years old, Vladimir Rakhmanov, together with his comrades, was moving steadily closer to the Pole—tortured by the lack of sleep, the monotony, the white mist. When it became almost unbearable he would remember the start from Henrietta and the first days of the trek. These memories made the going easier. It could not be worse than those days in March; the most difficult and dangerous part was already behind them. All he had to do now was put up with it, that was all. Put up with it and trudge onward.

It was certainly no coincidence that his thoughts returned to those first days—for him the start was the most grueling test. No one knew about the notes Rakhmanov made on March 23, the eighth day of the journey: "After lunch I finally came to, and believed that I could live amid the ice for quite a long time. What happened I do not know, but up until then it was simply unbearable. Even now my rucksack weighs on me terribly, and my feet and hands are freezing, but this has now become what might be called 'a normal perception of hardships.' "

At Dmitri's suggestion, Yuri and Vladimir began setting up the theodolite during the ten-minute breaks. "It's useless," Rakhmanov at first protested feebly, but when Yuri supported the idea, he stopped grumbling and in his usual conscientious way got down to business.

And still there was no sun. . . .

On May 26 they decided: if by tomorrow they were unable to pinpoint their position, then they would discontinue their "groping in the dark." They would pitch camp and wait for the sun.

The following day was even more overcast. They trudged on until the lunch break, as if all of them had forgotten their decision. They had their lunch in the tent.

"Well," asked Dmitri. "What do we do now?"

"Shall we keep on going?"

They rose to their feet, struck camp, and silently moved on. To sit around and wait until Nature showed mercy, to sit around doing nothing—this was not for them.

In the meantime, events were developing on the mainland. By the end of May throngs of journalists, photographers, and TV crews had zeroed in on Chersky. That small settlement at the mouth of the Kolyma River had never seen so many celebrities, and probably never will again. The famous Soviet poet Andrei Voznesensky; an associate of Thor Heyerdahl; the physician-explorer Yuri Senkevich; the journalist and Lenin Prize Winner Vasili Peskov; various legendary polar explorers and famous authors—all had flown in from Moscow to meet these conquerors of the North Pole. All of them eagerly awaited the signal to board the plane and fly to NP-24. From there the lucky ones would continue on to the Pole. The signal was to be a radio message from the skiers that they had finally reached their goal.

We had all until recently been of the opinion that if the skiers kept up the pace they had set during the early days of May, it would not be long. Who would have thought that at this point the Arctic would steal the sun from the sky?

And so the Moscow celebrities were forced to while away the time at Chersky's tiny hotel, much to the delight of the local inhabitants.

In the suite reserved for headquarters staff was a telephone with a hot line to Moscow—and this telephone seemed never to stop ringing. In the capital they could not understand the reason for the delay. Everyone seemed to be nagging us. "When are they going to get there?" they all kept asking.

For hours on end Obukhov and I sat in front of the local ham radio station, making contact first with the group and then with NP-24. Each day the group reported the same thing: "No sun. Unable to determine our coordinates." Not until the evening of May 27, did we hear what we had all been waiting for: "Take down our coordinates: 89°28' north latitude, 160° west longitude."

"Roger!" I exclaimed happily. "Only the latitude is not west, but east, right? That *was* a slip of the tongue, wasn't it?"

"Vladimir," Shparo said in a tired voice two thousand kilometers away, "it was no slip of the tongue. West latitude, you hear me, west! Do you read me?"

I read him, all right, but I can't say I understood it. How had they wound up in the Western Hemisphere? For two and a half months the group had marched toward its goal almost directly along the 160th meridian east longitude, north from Siberia, and now it turned out they were approaching the Pole from the Alaskan side. Was I hallucinating? Were they?

"It seems that during the past few days, when we were unable to fix our position, we were moving west instead of north, sort of circling the Pole," Dmitri explained. "So we made a slight detour. Now we've made the necessary navigational corrections, but the sun has disappeared again. So we may run into some more difficulties."

During those days it was the pilots who were most nervous. Theirs was a very complicated task: they had to fly several light planes to the Pole and back. Never before in the history of the Arctic had single-engine aircraft flown to the area around the Pole in late spring or summer. To facilitate the operation, an intermediate base had to be set up halfway between NP-24 and the Pole, so that the planes could refuel. Every day of delay complicated the operation even more: as summer approached, the weather became drastically worse, the ice fields more rare—and flights and landings became increasingly risky. I could well understand the pilots and the pleading looks they sent our way.

On May 29 an IL-14 piloted by Oleg Okhonsky airlifted the anxious tribe of journalists and the welcoming party to NP-24. I had flown there a few hours earlier. The station now resembled a small-town airport in bad weather. Next to the houses stood five AN-2s, while a little further on two IL-14s were tucked away in the "pocket." Dozens of men in city clothes strolled around the icefloe practically around the clock. Because there were not enough bunks to accommodate them, these people had to sleep in shifts, and were a bit bleary-eyed as a result. The population of NP-24 had mushroomed overnight: there were about thirty people in the welcoming party, forty airmen, staff members from expedition headquarters, journalists. . . . For a few days at least, NP-24 was a real boomtown.

The temperature at the station hovered around minus ten. It was snowing.

Following are some entries from my diary.

May 29. At 0100 Moscow time I made radio contact with the group. Dmitri has asked our base radio station to operate on reception mode continuously, beginning at 0600 hours. They are unable to determine their coordinates and have once again detected a strong head-on drift.

From Chersky we got the weather forecast for the next twenty-four hours: a low-pressure zone from Spitsbergen is traveling toward the Pole. Winds of up to fifteen meters per second are expected, and visibility will be restricted to one kilometer. Another little gift from Mother Nature.

At 1230 the five AN-2s took off into the murky sky and headed northward. Their mission was to find a suitable icefloe about five hundred kilometers distant, make a landing, and leave barrels of fuel. We know that the crews of these planes are made up of the finest polar

233

flyers, yet we are a bit uneasy just the same. An atmosphere of anxious waiting reigned at NP-24.

The daytime radio contact with the ski team yielded no news that could be considered good. Once again Shparo complained of the cloudy weather and head-on drift. An emergency procedure for reaching the Pole was discussed: an AN-2, with the aid of its navigational instruments, would find the Pole, make a landing there, and then like a beacon send out radio signals for the group to pick up and home in on. This option is not entirely out of the question, although Dmitri thinks people may criticize them if they take it, claiming that they had not found the Pole by themselves, but had been led there like blind kittens.

At 1700 a message was received from the group commander of the AN-2s: the intermediate base had been organized and four Annies were flying back to NP-24. The fifth, according to plan, stayed behind to serve as a radio beacon. Three hours later we all gave a hefty cheer when the four planes appeared in the sky above the station. The Annies flew in tight formation, as if on parade—an impressive spectacle here in the heart of the Arctic.

The schedule for the ski team was now as follows: five hours of forced march alternating with two hours of rest. The skiers were working practically round the clock. There was no sense now trying to conserve their energy; the idea was to reach the Pole as soon as possible.

At 2200, on one of their rest stops, Anatoli radioed that they had managed to "catch" the sun and fix their position. They were less than forty kilometers away from the Pole. "Do you hear any squeaking yet?" I asked Melnikov. He immediately got my joke. "No," he said, "we can't even see the earth's axis yet. Possibly we may stumble across it beyond that distant hummock." That little joke dates back to Papanin's expedition, yet it continues to circulate among those who have been at the Pole, or near it. That it is not worn out from overuse hardly needs saying. The North Pole will never become a mecca for tourists as, say, the South Pole might. There the ice sits on solid land, a pole has been erected on the spot, and you can get your photograph taken standing next to it. The Amundsen-Scott scientific station is there to offer warmth, food, and lodging for visitors. But up here there is neither pole, nor lodgings, nor solid land. Here the Arctic Ocean is 4,033 meters deep, and it is covered with a tattered quilt of drifting icefloes.

May 30. At 0950 Shparo was on the air.

"We've made little progress," he said sourly. "The ice is bad, the weather is bad. Our latitude is 89°59' north."

"You're practically there," I tried to cheer him up. "We have the following plan: today at 2200 hours the base-camp participants in the expedition, including Obukhov and myself, will fly on board two Annies to the intermediate base. There we'll set up our radio station and await your report on reaching the Pole. After that we fly out to you."

"When will it be 2200?"

"Half a day," I replied, not at all surprised by the question, since I knew that with the ski team there was plenty of confusion regarding the correct time. They lived on local time (that is, the Yakutsk Time Zone), while during their navigational operations they used Greenwich Mean Time. In addition, the times for their radio sessions were given in Moscow time, and they had to take into account also the time used at NP-24 (Moscow time) plus twelve hours.

"The only thing I ask is that you give us time to calmly reach our goal, to precisely determine the site of the Pole," Dmitri said. "Let's not bungle the finish. Do not fly out to the Pole without our consent."

"Don't worry. There's no way we'll fly to the Pole before you get there."

"All right, Vladimir. That's it for the time being. I want a half-hour's sleep."

I remember the great pleasure I felt while reading a book by the British explorer, Wally Herbert, who with three of his companions made a trans-Arctic journey by sled some ten years ago. Herbert, like many of his predecessors, devoted a lot of space to describing his efforts to locate the Pole. He emphasized that navigation in close proximity to the Pole is a complicated problem. The slightest inaccuracy in determining the longitude, and you make a mistake in fixing the moment the sun crosses your meridian. In the end you start going around in circles.

At 2235 Labutin, Sklokin, Ivanov, Deyev, Shatokhin, Obukhov, and myself flew out of NP-24 on two Annies. We had with us a powerful radio set for direct contact with Moscow, as well as for Labutin to operate at the exact point of the Pole the final day of the ham radio competition. The weather was miserable. As our plane penetrated the cloud cover, its wings became covered with ice. The captain got worried and almost turned back.

There is no sense quoting my diary any longer. From this point on the entries were made hastily and are often illegible. Nor is it easy to fully recollect my personal impressions regarding the events of May 31 and June 1. It is difficult to say what feelings predominated: a sudden onset of extreme fatigue (as when an athlete crosses the finish line); intense happiness and joy (they made it!); or relief (they finally made it). Most probably, all this taken together.

And so, on May 31 at 0130 the two Annies touched down at the intermediate base. In half an hour, right there on the ice, under the open sky, we rigged up the radio equipment and Labutin went on the air. The first thing he did was call Moscow. Much to our surprise, our Moscow radio operator, Tenyakshev, responded at once. "Leonid, it's me," he said in a casual sort of tone, as if he were sitting behind a neighboring hummock instead of eight thousand kilometers away. The pilots, who up till then had looked with misgiving upon Labutin's little radio station, now made no effort to conceal their admiration. After finishing his talk with Moscow, Leonid, just for interest's sake, asked over the airwaves who else was on that frequency. And that's when bedlam broke loose. Murmansk, Sverdlovsk, Leningrad, Odessa, Yerevan, Tashkent. . . . And it was way past midnight in all those cities. Japanese and Canadian stations responded. There was even a call from Doncho Papazov, who with his wife Julia was sailing by yacht across the Pacific. It was as if every ham in the world was at that moment monitoring the air, in hopes of being the first to hear the news that the seven valiant skiers had conquered the North Pole.

In order to satisfy their curiosity, Labutin described the situation where he was.

"We are on an icefloe a meter and a half thick. Nearby there are three AN-2 aircraft, a ridge of newly formed hummocks. The radio is sitting on a plastic table; to one side a gasoline-powered generator is providing electricity for the radio set. There's a slight snowfall; temperature, minus 11; a white mist. In general, the whole atmosphere is quite exotic."

I got tired of trying to stay awake. Making it to the nearest aircraft, I crawled in, flopped down on some sacks, and went out like a light. It seemed like only a minute, but two hours had gone by when Shatokhin yelled right into my ear: "Get up! Dmitri is on the air. The Pole is ours!" Automatically, I looked at my watch: it was 0510 hours. I sprang to my feet and ran as fast as I could to the radio station.

Labutin was surrounded by everyone at the intermediate base. He was all smiles.

I grabbed the microphone. Forgetting all the rules of radio communication, dispensing with my call signals, I

237

yelled into the microphone: "Dmitri! Dmitri! Congratulations! It's a great victory! The Pole is ours!"

Yuri Khmelevsky was later to describe the final moments: "We had at that point lost all track of time. We marched for five hours, then rested, though Rakhmanov and I got practically no sleep during these stops—we were constantly on the lookout for the sun. For three days the group followed this punishing schedule. Reluctantly, it seemed, but inexorably, the Pole came nearer and nearer. On May 30 only a few kilometers stood between us and the Pole. Once again I got unlucky and took a dip in the ocean. By now, however, this had become so commonplace that no one made any comments. Ledenev was even happy about it, as he had finally managed to film a 'swim' for his movie. We continued walking for eight hours without stopping. It was by now May 31, and by every calculation, we were at the Pole.

"At 0245 we stopped in front of a large hummock and pitched the tent. Using our ski poles to rig a mast, we raised the red flag.

"Everyone felt he should behave in some special, solemn way. But how? Everyone seemed to be waiting for something to happen. Finally Dmitri said: 'Okay, men, let's stand next to each other in a tight circle and embrace each other's shoulders.' We silently grabbed hold of each other and this is when we felt it: that's it . . . period . . . it's over . . . the Pole . . . victory. . . . No one said a word, no one except Dmitri, who said very simply, 'We've reached our goal.' I felt a kind of stinging feeling in my eyes. Then I saw tears running down the cheeks of all the others. We stood there hugging each other, then began swaying to and fro in unison.

"I was happy not because I had made it to the Pole on skis, but because my friends, my companions, were there next to me. I felt especially close to all of them at

238

that moment. We had made it to the Pole! The seven of us.

"Vadim fired his carbine into the air ten times. 'Salute!' he exclaimed. 'For Shapro! For Khemelevsky! For Ledenev! For Melnikov! For Rakhmanov! For Shishkarev! For Davydov! For victory! For victory! For victory!'

"Then we contacted the intermediate base and, waiting for your arrival, fell sound asleep."

At 0600 we took off from the intermediate base. At 1000 hours we spotted their tent. Senior navigator Victor Krivosheya, having finished his calculations, confirmed: "That's it, all right—that's the Pole!"

It proved impossible to make a landing next to the camp—there was no suitable icefloe—so we came down about one kilometer from the tent on a large piece of fresh ice. It was the size of three football fields and about fifty centimeters thick. I climbed up on top of the plane's fuselage and in the distance, behind a ridge of hummocks, could make out the contours of seven small figures headed in our direction. We set out to meet them.

As the distance between us shortened, both groups began walking faster and faster. Then everyone broke into a run.

From the sidelines it must have looked strange: two groups of people running toward each other—sinking into the deep snow, falling, stumbling, short of breath. And all around them a white plain studded with blue hummocks. A low grey sky. A great silence.

We will meet in a few minutes, I thought to myself. But first I wanted to look with wide-open eyes into the faces of my friends, trying to detect in them the traces of their long journey, something that would single them out from other people. And then we could hug each other and go circling in some silly merry-go-round, like people out of their minds, rolling around in the snow. . . .

We would meet in just a few more minutes. And then the planes would bring in the journalists and the cameramen. There would be a solemn moment while we raised the state flag of the USSR. Speeches. A ceremony. Official protocols would be signed. A football game at the Pole between the old-timers and the greenhorns. (Afterwards Vasili Shishkarev would sit down to write his father a letter: "You were always annoyed with me for not continuing my studies, for taking up strange jobs, and, in general, being a good-for-nothing. A higher education is by no means synonymous with higher human qualities. Man's main goal is to be a Man. And in this respect you raised me properly. Not many people have been at the North Pole, though many have tried. Very few have reached the Pole on their own. And only seven men in the whole wide world have reached the Pole on skis. Among them was your son.")

Very soon, I thought, right over that last ridge of hummocks, we will finish our long run toward each other. And for a split second we may experience a feeling of sorrow that the goal we have been striving toward for ten years has finally been reached.

In the days to come there would be a round of heroes' welcomes on the mainland. Decorations. Articles in newspapers and magazines. The trip to London. Long months of work on the expedition's scientific report. A brilliant presentation to the Academy of Sciences. And new journeys to the North. And new plans.

But in the meantime we were running toward each other at the North Pole.